COR

D1639506

UNIVERSITY OF BRADFORD
Library

BD 012832601 9

C 954.031/COR

BRADFORD INSTITUTE
OF TECHNOLOGY
HALL OF
RESIDENCE
LIBRARY

of that time disperse us into different parts
of the World, by which means it will almost
impossible to transact that affair; but on
the other hand if the payment should admitt
of any difficulty, tho' we as a collective body
are of some little weight, dispersed we dwindle
to nothing, and cannot in that situation
inforce any thing. the case cannot admitt
of those difficulties in regard to the Company,
for by your means their affairs are settled
on a stronger foundation than ever, and
therefore by keeping up a sufficient Force here
they will always be able to make good any
Security which the Nabob at present can
give them.
　　　　　　　　In this perhaps We may
appear to be a little too sanguine, as even
half the money promised is a great sum to
men in our situations. true Sir. but the
promise which was made us at setting out,
joined to the success which our arms have met
with, has led us to the flattering idea of gaining
　　　　　　　　　　　　　　　　considerable

MAJOR JOHN CORNEILLE

Journal of my Service in India

EDITED WITH AN INTRODUCTION
BY MICHAEL EDWARDES
ILLUSTRATIONS BY B. S. BIRO

THE FOLIO SOCIETY
LONDON · MCMLXVI

© The Folio Society Ltd 1966
The binding design is from an engraving of
Fort St George, Madras, made *c.* 1757.
The frontispiece shows a page from
Major Corneille's manuscript.
The endpapers show the arms of
George II and The East India Company.
Map drawn by K. C. Jordan.

BRADFORD INSTITUTE OF TECHNOLOGY
LIBRARY
13 MAY 1966

ACCESSION No.	CLASS No.
~~RESERVED~~ 128326	C 954·031

LOCATION

PRINTED IN GREAT BRITAIN
Set in 11 point Baskerville 2 points leaded and
printed by Richard Clay (The Chaucer Press) Ltd
Bungay Suffolk
Frontispiece printed by Jarrold and Sons Ltd, Norwich
Bound by W & J Mackay Ltd Chatham

CONTENTS

PART TWO

INTRODUCTION

When John Corneille arrived in India in 1754, he found the English still only merchants and traders, anxious over their profit. When he left, just over three years later, those same merchants were assuming the role of empire-builders and setting off—with some reluctance and foreboding—upon the conquest of India. They did so, not in the name of the king of England, but in that of the Directors of The United Company of Merchants of England trading to the East Indies, with offices in Leadenhall Street, London. This Company, confirmed by a charter from Queen Anne in 1708, had been created by the amalgamation of two East India companies, one of which had first received its charter from Queen Elizabeth in 1600 to trade in such exotic luxuries as spices, gems, bezoar stones, indigo, camphor and sulphur. By the beginning of the eighteenth century, trade had expanded to include such things as fine muslins and calicoes, tea and coffee.

The English, of course, were not the only traders in India. The Portuguese—the first Europeans to establish themselves there—had been displaced from their trading monopoly by the Dutch, who took over the lucrative pepper trade for themselves. In fact, the first of the two English companies had been established in order to break the Dutch monopoly in spices. The French Compagnie des Indes had also opened trading stations in India as, on a much smaller scale, had the Danes and the Imperial Ostend Company. The rivalry between the various companies was the rivalry between business houses. Each intrigued with native rulers and tried to outwit the others, but at the beginning of the eighteenth century all the Europeans still respected the prestige of the ageing Mughal emperor, Aurangzeb, and lived in considerable fear of the Mughal provincial governors.

The principal English settlements in India were at Madras (Fort St George), Calcutta (Fort William), Surat and Bombay. There were other, smaller centres in Bengal and on the coasts of Malabar and Coromandel, one being Fort St David opposite the town of Cuddalore, a hundred miles south of Madras. It was at Fort St David that Corneille was first to learn something of India and of the merchants who represented the United Company.

Life in the English settlements was, on Corneille's arrival, still very much as it had been at the beginning of the century though some changes had taken place, and were still taking place, under the pressure of events. The administration was strictly paternal in character. The governor, or president as he was called at Madras, was usually the senior merchant. He achieved his appointment not by merit but by longevity, having survived other merchants, over-eating, and the tropical climate. To support him, there was a council made up of the other senior merchants of the settlement.

The governor had both commercial and political functions. His first duty, however, was to the Company and the Company's business. In Council, he had only a casting vote, and no authority to over-rule its members. He was treated with intense suspicion by the Directors in London and was liable to be dismissed on such flimsy evidence as allegations contained in private letters to the Directors from members of his own council who were anxious to blacken his character. Consequently, many of the men who accepted the position of governor were either inhibited or made arrogant by anxiety, according to their temperament.

As head of the settlement, however, representing the king of England and negotiating with native princes and rulers, the governor received a larger salary, had more splendid living accommodation and displayed some pomp. One such governor had a bodyguard of eighty armed peons as well as English soldiers; two flags were carried in front of him; and his journeys were accompanied, as one traveller recorded, by 'country musick enough to frighten a stranger into belief the men were mad'.

Below the governor, the Company hierarchy was severely defined, each man moving through the grades of Writer, Factor, Junior and Senior Merchant—if he survived the climate and his way of life. In some of the settlements there were a number of 'free' merchants, i.e. merchants outside the Company's employ. Where these were numerous, as in Madras, they elected a mayor and aldermen. The Mayor's Court had the right to try civil and criminal cases, and the president and his council acted as a court of appeal.

Usually, settlements were divided into a European area, including and surrounding the fort, and a Black Town where Indian merchants anxious to do business settled in increasing numbers. At the beginning of the eighteenth century, the number of Englishmen in India was still quite small; and most of the Company's employees lived within the fort, taking their meals at a common table. They ate and drank well—too well, in the context of the climate. Fifteen courses were not unusual at dinner, which was taken at midday, and they might include such delicacies as 'Kishmashes, Bengall Goats, Sugar Candy, Almonds, Brahminy Bull, Soyce, Turkeys, Geese, Rabbits, and Lime'. Vast quantities of local and imported wines and spirits were consumed. A heavy meat diet and immense meals, washed down with wine and taken in the heat of the day, kept mortality rates high. The corporate life of the settlement was, however, beginning to be eroded by the arrival of English women, though these were still few in number even in the middle of the century. As there were not enough women to go round, and as their choice obviously fell on the more senior merchants, the junior factors and writers still lived together.

Until 1746 and the first war between the English and the French in India, the Company's military forces were only a sort of armed constabulary intended to protect buildings and goods and keep some measure of law and order. The settlement garrison consisted of Europeans, 'black Mungrel Portuguese', half-castes and peons. And according to one visitor to Madras, 'each soldier kept his Boy, who tho' not more than ten years old, is Procurer and Valet de Chambre'. Duties were not arduous, consisting of guarding the gates of the fort and patrolling the streets at night.

In fact, the European population had very little with which to occupy its mind. Life was dull and boredom an insistent enemy. The richer merchants could, and did, build themselves garden houses in salubrious spots in the surrounding countryside, but for their juniors there was little else to do but stroll in the open spaces of the town and gossip in the taverns and punch-houses. Gambling was the principal sport and reached such levels that the Company ordered that any person in its employ found gaming for a sum higher than ten pounds was to be instantly dismissed and sent home to England. This did not reduce gambling but it did encourage discretion amongst the players.

Generally speaking, the English kept apart from Indian life, though they had no racial prejudices and certainly no contempt for Indian customs. They were happy to take over from the Indians anything which made life pleasanter or more luxurious, from food and clothes to the institution of the *zenana*. They did not bother to learn Indian languages but carried on communication in the demotic Portuguese which was the *lingua franca* of the coasts, or through interpreters. The Englishman lived comfortably in the country, but remained an Englishman at heart. Changes were, however, taking place. Two events, two catastrophes, were to accelerate them.

The first of these was the capture of Madras by the French in 1746, and the second—whose consequences were to involve Corneille—the capture of Calcutta by Siraj-ud-daula, the Nawab of Bengal, ten years later.

The attack on Madras was an offshoot of the war in Europe between France and England, known as the War of the Austrian Succession. Both the French and English in India tried to keep the war confined to Europe but the French home government was determined to strike a blow at the British in India and sent a naval force which captured Madras before it had to retire, damaged by a hurricane, to Mauritius. Then, in June 1748, an English fleet appeared and laid siege to Pondicherry, the principal French settlement. The onset of the monsoon, however, and the inferior military skill of the English compelled them to raise the siege. Before the war could be resumed, peace was signed in Europe. Madras was handed back to the English, and the fleet sailed for home.

The first effect of the French wars was to bring a sudden growth of military forces in the English settlements in South India. Royal troops—i.e. units of the British Army—first arrived in India at the close of the War of the Austrian Succession. At this time, too, the Company, realising that it needed regular troops of its own, also began to raise European regiments to replace the old military police.

The Company, whether it liked it or not—and it did not —was forced by its military operations against the French to enter Indian politics. The reason for this can be found in the state of India at the time. After the death of

Aurangzeb in 1707, the Mughal empire had begun to decline. The governors of the old Mughal provinces, through a mixture of personal ambition and contempt for a succession of weak emperors, began to assert their independence, to make themselves the rulers of the provinces they had originally held on behalf of the emperor. In 1739, the Emperor Muhammad Shah virtually handed his empire over to the Persian invader, Nadir Shah. The year before, the Marathas—who had been threatening the empire even before the death of Aurangzeb—had cut the Mughal possessions in two. They, in fact, inherited most of the Mughal power and by 1750, their dominions —centred on Poona—stretched from the west coast to the Bay of Bengal and from the banks of the river Ganges to the borders of Mysore. The Marathas now occupied the core of India; on the periphery were Oudh, Bengal, Hyderabad and the Carnatic, independent under their former Mughal governors.

The French and the English each sought alliances amongst the native rulers. In doing so, they involved themselves in strictly Indian intrigues. What had begun as a purely defensive measure against the French was to draw the English into the vortex of Indian politics. Merchants were soon forced—not altogether against their will, after they realised the financial advantages—to become soldiers and politicians. The increase in the military establishment, the climate of adventure enhanced by political and military success, released all their ambitions for wealth long suppressed by a feeling of insecurity in the face of Indian power. Opportunity thundered at their doors and every man tried his best to turn it to his own advantage. But in becoming soldiers and statesmen, the English merchants never forgot their commercial training. There was a price for everything. Newcomers soon learned how to make a profit. Captains were eager to accept contracts for clothing and feeding their companies; colonels pocketed the pay of non-existent soldiers. There was even a whole regiment which, when the time came for its disbandment, was found to exist only on paper.

The coming of the soldiers in fairly large numbers began after 1748. In that year, twelve hastily raised companies and eight artillerymen were landed in Madras from the fleet of Admiral Boscawen. But the first complete royal regiment to land in India was the 39th, commanded by Colonel Adlercron and numbering amongst its officers John Corneille. After that, the numbers increased steadily throughout the rest of the eighteenth century. Royal officers were free from the niggling control of the Company's Directors in London. They were inclined to despise the Company's servants because they were traders, and the officers of the Company's army because they were traders in uniform—concerned not with glory, honour and fame, but with increasing the profit of their Honourable masters in Leadenhall Street. The Company's European troops, in fact, were of poor quality, but the royal officers themselves were not altogether uninterested in personal profit. Affairs in Bengal brought it to many of them.

The new military forces, both royal and Company's, altered very considerably the balance of the English population in India. Where, in the first half of the century, most of that population had been in the Company's service and predominantly mercantile in preoccupation, the second half saw these men outnumbered by professional soldiers. Of the new arrivals, those employed in the Company's own forces came out for life or for very long periods, and they imbibed much of the social habit and commercial spirit of the merchants who were their masters. Royal officers, on the other hand, stayed in India for a comparatively short time and considered their tour of duty there as only an inter-lude—albeit a potentially profitable one—in their military career.

The battle of Plassey, in purely military terms an insignifi-cant affair, also brought about great changes in the lives and attitudes of the English civilians in India. The con-quest of Bengal released the English from the ghetto of their trading stations and their forts. Before 1750 the few Company servants who made a fortune in India had returned to England and invested their money in land, just as if they had made an ordinary commercial fortune in England. After Plassey, when English administrators spread out into the countryside and came in contact with the luxury and ostentation of the Indian aristocracy, the returning Englishman became anxious for social position, titles and political influence. After Plassey, the 'nabobs'—as they came to be called in England—displayed the ex-travagance and pomp which they had learned in India. They entered the English parliament in force after the election of 1768 and from then onwards formed a powerful political lobby.

The English nabobs owed their fortunes, or at least the opportunity of acquiring them, almost entirely to the activities of Robert Clive. Though he towered above his contemporaries, Clive was perhaps the most character-istic figure of these times of change. Starting life as a merchant, he had become a soldier-politician and finally an empire-builder. The character of Clive has been either fulsomely praised or viciously abused. One modern Indian historian, for example, has called him 'a gangster who had achieved glory, a confessed forger, liar and cheat, whose military achievements compared with those of the generals of the time were wholly ridiculous'. This judge-ment is not completely wrong, but it is not wise to judge

Clive or any other man of the eighteenth century, in Europe or in India, by the moral standards of a nunnery. Clive proceeded with the same ruthlessness as the Indian princes of his time, which was not far removed from that of the princes and politicians of Europe. In the field of military achievement, Plassey was certainly no classic general's battle. It was won by a combination of intrigue and audacity. The army of the Nawab of Bengal had already been sapped by conspiracy. William Watts, acting as Clive's agent, had bought Mir Jafar with the promise that the British would make him nawab. But as the troops of Clive and Siraj-ud-daula moved closer together, Clive was still not sure of Mir Jafar. Even when the battle of Plassey had actually begun, Clive—as far as he knew was confronted by a vast force of some 35,000 infantry, 15,000 cavalry and a large number of guns under the command of a Frenchman. Facing this, Clive had less than 3000 men, the majority of whom were Indians. But even though the Nawab's generals were divided, or in pursuit of personal gain, Plassey was a real victory and a victory for European military science. The native armies of India were badly led, ill-trained, without discipline. All they had was large numbers, and in a rout this merely increased the confusion. Clive's little force was disciplined and directed by European experience, and it demonstrated once and for all that a small body of properly trained men, led by European officers, could defeat the raggle-taggle mob of a native army.

The psychological effects of the victory of Plassey were immense. The measure of Clive's achievement can easily be made by comparing the position of the British in Bengal in 1756 and in 1760. In 1756 the British were merely merchants, prosperous ones, of course, but still only traders sharing the commerce permitted to them by the Nawab of Bengal with the French and other Europeans.

The British would never have thought of challenging the Nawab if Siraj-ud-daula himself had not attacked and captured Calcutta from them. He did so partly to satisfy his own pride and avarice, partly because he had come to fear that one day the English might attack him—a belief assiduously fostered by the French in order to advance their own commercial interests.

In 1760, the situation was very different. Mir Jafar, the new Nawab, was a puppet of Robert Clive and was soon to be discarded by the puppet-master. French influence in Bengal was at an end. The Dutch, foolishly challenging the British after Plassey, were easily defeated in 1759. Having tasted the profits of conquest, the British began to extend their influence outwards into India. When Madras was once again threatened by the French, it was the rich possession of Bengal that enabled the British to fight back and defeat them. In 1764, the merchants who had once been interested only in quiet trade defeated the Mughal emperor and his allies at the battle of Buxar, the first battle in their conquest of the whole of India.

To this rapidly changing and exotic world of mid-eighteenth century India, John Corneille brought an un-prejudiced and objective eye. This in itself should not be thought remarkable. The eighteenth century was a par-ticularly tolerant age. No man despised another because of his colour. Thoughts of racial superiority were still over the horizon—although Corneille was slightly surprised to find that 'black' girls could be described as beautiful even by European standards. Never having seen a 'black' girl before leaving home, however, his surprise was the pro-duct rather of inexperience than of prejudice. His descrip-tions of places, people and things are sensible and accurate, his judgement of his fellow officers and of the Company's servants acute and informed.

John Corneille belonged to a military family. His father, of Swiss origin, became a major in the British service. His brother, Edward, also served in the British Army. The author of this journal was born about the year 1727 and entered the Army when he was little more than a boy. He joined the 39th regiment (later known as 'The Dorsetshire') at the beginning of 1754, after being on half-pay with the 61st. At this time, he was a lieutenant. He was promoted captain-lieutenant in 1759, captain in 1760 and major in 1768, and finally retired from the service in 1772. Another John Corneille, presumably the author's son or nephew, is recorded as being a captain in the 39th regiment in 1795.

In preparing the manuscript, which has only recently been discovered in France, I have altered very little. Corneille's work, which is in the form of a long letter to his father, has been divided into convenient chapters; some rather involved sentences have been simplified; and the spelling of certain words has been modernised. Where clarification has been called for, this has been inserted within square brackets. Indian names are given first in Corneille's own rule-of-thumb transliteration, followed by the correct and modern spelling, also in square brackets; this modern spelling is used on all subsequent occasions. An exception to this has been made in the treatment of documents quoted by Corneille, which have been left with their original form, spelling and punctuation.

MICHAEL EDWARDES

B

TO MY FATHER

Sir,

The pleasure which I am informed you have expressed with the accounts I hitherto sent of my voyage has induced me, in the leisure of my returning home, to exert my memory in collecting, amplifying, and connecting the several epistles I have written since the first of the expedition, in order that you may have before you at one view a fuller and more satisfactory idea of the public and private transactions in which your son was any way concerned.

As it is entirely the foregoing reason that has led me to this undertaking, and no premeditated design from the first of the expedition, I have neglected taking memorials of many things that would have embellished such a narrative, but the motive of the undertaking will, I hope, excuse the errors.

PART
ONE

CHAPTER ONE

The little dependence that military men ought to have of being fixed in any place—nay, kingdom—for any length of time, and the necessity they live under of being ready at short warning to go where their duty may call them, was never better exemplified than by this expedition. It was undertaken when the peace that was then established in Europe might have seemed to promise not action but tranquillity, rest and ease; and the time allowed for preparation was exceedingly short considering the length of the voyage.

On 29 January 1754, the Duke of Dorset, then Lord Lieutenant of Ireland, informed Colonel Adlercron that our regiment had been fixed on by His Majesty to embark for the East Indies and that it was to be brought up immediately—by drafts from the different regiments then in the kingdom of Ireland—to a strength of three sergeants, three corporals, two drummers and seventy privates per company, with three additional surgeon's mates. The regiment was to be ready by 1 March to embark on board a fleet which would by that time be at Cork to receive it. Colonel Adlercron received this news with the appearance of cheerful resignation which every man who takes the profession of arms ought to be able to command; for though insensibility is by no means a disposition one would be at pains to acquire, yet the semblance of it is at times absolutely necessary.

The colonel repaired with all despatch to London, and there he found that HRH [The Duke of Cumberland, son of George II and victor of Culloden] had been to the trouble of finding out the characters of each officer in the regiment, a knowledge he made use of to supplant those whom he regarded as unfit, because of sickness or other reasons, for such an expedition. His precaution cannot be too much commended; were it exerted upon all occasions of this kind, it would generally ensure the success of the undertaking.

The colonel despatched his affairs in London, returned to Dublin, and joined the regiment at Cork about the 14 March. The fleet intended for the expedition had already arrived at Kinsale, commanded by Admiral Watson. It consisted of the *Kent* of sixty guns, the *Eagle*, also of sixty, the *Bristol*, fifty, the *Salisbury*, fifty, the *Bridgewater*, twenty, and the *Kingfisher*, a sloop of war. Unavoidable delays, which obliged the fleet to remain there somewhat longer than expected, might have wrecked matters entirely, for a gale of wind from the south-east threatened the *Eagle* and the *Bristol* which were not far enough within the harbour. It lasted but a short time, however, and they escaped with only having to cut away their masts. This hastened rather than retarded us, and on 23 March part of the regiment set off from Cork for Kinsale in order to embark. The detachment destined for the two disabled ships remained until the ships were sufficiently refitted to sail to Plymouth, where the *Cumberland* and *Tyger*—the former of seventy, the latter of sixty guns—were ready to replace them.

Both sailors and soldiers were transferred into them and they proceeded on the voyage.

As the men-of-war were not sufficient to carry the whole of the regiment as well as a detachment of artillery consisting of about seventy men, with twelve short sixes [short-barrelled six-pounder guns] and stores in proportion, three [East] India [Company] ships had also been ordered to attend at Cork: the *Kent*, the *London*, and the *Britannia*. The latter was my lot. As we sailed alone, I shall confine the account of an East India voyage to the particular occurrences that fell under my observation.

We intended sailing on the 26th but, not being able to purchase our anchor for the morning's tide, we deferred our departure until the next day, which gave us the opportunity of witnessing a remarkable instance of love and resolution on the part of the wife of one of our corporals. The poor creature, passionately fond of her husband and loath to leave him, hoped that by disguising herself in the habit of a sailor she might remain unnoticed for some days and thus make the voyage with him. But the soldiers, finding out, told the captain of the ship who immediately sent for the woman and taxed her with this information. At first she absolutely denied it as false and groundless, but it was her misfortune that the sexes are too easily distinguishable! A demand to see her bosom obliged her to acknowledge that she had disguised herself in expectation of accompanying her husband—whom else, she said with tears, she never expected to see more. The distressed situation of the poor creature seemed to move all those who were present and we made a collection of about twenty shillings and sent her safe ashore without enquiring if the husband was privy to the plot. This, with other scenes of distress, in which officers as well as soldiers were involved, showed me my profession in a most doleful light and led me to reflect that it is as well that young men

choose their way of life while their judgement is still un-
formed, else it is probable that the necessary evil of the
press-gang would not be confined to the navy alone.

We left the cove of Cork on Wednesday, 27 March
1754, on board the *Britannia*, an Indiaman of eight
hundred tons commanded by Captain Nevil Norway, and a
brisk gale from the north-east drove us along at a rate of
ten knots an hour. Its effect was soon visible on most
persons on the ship and on myself in particular, for I was
extremely sick that day and part of the next. With the
help of some mulled claret, however, my stomach became
composed and I entirely got the better of seasickness.

My first night I passed most disagreeably. Fatigued both
in body and mind, I had expected to find some little rest
in my hammock, but about four o'clock—because of the
rocking of the ship and the fact that my swinging bed was
unskilfully tied—down I fell, bed and all, from a height of
five feet and with a most unmerciful thump. It was then
that I lost my naturally phlegmatic temper, cursed my
profession, my servant, the sea, the wind, nay, almost
myself, and a thousand times gave preference over my
condition to the poorest labourer in the poorest cottage.
After my passion had subsided, I began to hearken to
reason, got my hammock tied once more, went to bed,
and slept the remainder of the night pretty well.

To me, entirely unacquainted with life at sea, it appeared extraordinary that so many creatures could be
crammed into this wooden world. In all, we were 237
men, with livestock and provisions of all kinds in great
abundance laid in at the expense of the [East India]
Company. We had a good table, and very good order kept
on board. Our hours were early and exact; eight o'clock
breakfast, twelve dinner, eight supper, to bed about ten,
and up at six. Thus, by regularity and temperance, we
expected to preserve our health notwithstanding the

length of our voyage and the many variations of climate
we would encounter.

Our favourable north-east wind continued until Monday, 1 April, when it left us in north latitude 36° 41'. After
this we had weak and variable winds, usually north-west
and south-west, and the weather in general was very fine
with almost continually bright sun and clear skies.
Nature was as pleasant as it can be where nothing but
the heavens and waters are to be seen. The heat was not
yet in any way inconvenient, it being no warmer than a
fine summer's day in Ireland.

The 3rd of April was ushered in with a most melancholy
accident. About six in the morning, one of the gunners
pulling up a bucket of salt water fell overboard. A rope
was immediately thrown, which reached him, but the
poor fellow being a bad swimmer and encumbered with a
greatcoat, was in so much confusion as not to be able to
catch it. Though a boat was let down in less than three
minutes, and though the day was fine and the sea calm,
yet he sank at about sixty yards' distance in view of all the
men on board. It was an introduction to the dangers of the
sea, and had at least this good effect, that it made our
landsmen more cautious than they were at first.

Early on the morning of the 7th, we came in sight of
the island of Madeira, which, from about five leagues'
distance, appeared to be very high land.

On the 8th, our dinner was disagreeably disturbed by
the loss of our fore-topmast and main-topgallant-mast.
It was supposed to be owing to some defect in the wood,
for at the time we had little wind and not much rolling.
Luckily no-one was hurt. Such are the comforts of a sea
life—never secure from some accident that may spoil a
good meal! As the weather continued very fine, our loss
was repaired by the next evening.

On the 10th we saw the island of Palma, one of the

Canaries, lying about fifteen leagues westward and the next day we came within eight leagues of it. It is prodigiously high and there was snow plainly discernible on its top though it was then quite warm at sea. On the 12th before sunrise we came within sight of the island of Ferra [Hierro], the most westerly of the Canaries, and could just perceive the peak of Teneriffe although it was then computed to be at least thirty leagues distant.

Next day most of the officers and men had themselves bled by way of precaution, as we were approaching the nearer visits of the sun. It is, I believe, needless when in perfect health; the only precaution to be recommended is abstemiousness in eating and drinking, and regularity in hours.

On Wednesday, 17 April, we fell in with a 'confirmed trade' in latitude 19° 8' north. This is a wind that blows constantly from the north-east or thereabouts in some of the degrees between the north Tropic and the Line. It is uncertain, even from the observations of experienced sailors, exactly where it will be met or for how long it will stay with a ship. We fell in with it late, and it left us in 9° 2' north, which was sooner than expected.

The first novelty one generally sees in these latitudes is the Tropic Bird [*Phaethon lepturus*, also known as the Bo'sun Bird] so called because it always keeps between the Tropic and the Line. Its body is little larger than a pigeon, of a whitish colour, and with a tail about nine inches long consisting of two feathers that terminate in a point. Flying fish we have here in abundance which, on the monotonous sea, afford us much amusement. They fly out of the water in shoals, pursued by bonitos and albacores, and are no sooner in the air than they become the prey of birds resembling our gulls. These fish somewhat resemble the herring. They are from four to seven inches long, and their fins—which also serve as wings—are fixed near the gills.

The fins are remarkable in being always the same length as the body. They usually fly about a hundred yards and then fall as if they had no power to go any further, which makes it seem that they can only fly as long as their fins are wet. They cannot see when out of the water, for several flew on board our ship.

Dolphin is another kind of fish particular to this part of the world. The body is made like a salmon but much longer, and the head is large, round and flat at the sides. Its colours when in the water are most beautiful, azure, yellow, red, and green, finely mixed and variegated according to how it moves. We ate some of them, but found the taste not equal to the beauty; and the colours soon vanish when the fish is dead. Sharks abound hereabouts. The reason assigned is that this is the route followed by ships engaged in the slave trade and the sharks are well fed on the carcasses of the poor wretches who die and are thrown overboard. We have seen seven or eight in a day, mostly six feet long. The head of this fish is broad and flat, with a wide mouth and two or sometimes three rows of teeth according to its age. The upper jaw projects beyond the lower by about five inches but, according to report, the shark has no need to turn on its back to take its prey. Two or three small fish constantly swim in front of this creature's mouth and are therefore called 'pilot fish', while another type, known as 'sucking fish' sticks to its body. We caught several sharks as food for the sailors, and curiosity made me taste it. It seems to me to resemble the ray. One shark which was caught by the *Cumberland* in her passage to the Indies had seventy-two young ones in her belly, each about fourteen inches in length.

Sharks are never seen but in calm weather which frequently occurs approaching the Line. We experienced it, as well as heavy rains, thunder and lightning. At such

times the heat is immoderate, depresses the spirits, and
renders one incapable of doing or applying oneself to
anything.

On the 29th we had a most violent squall which
occasioned the loss of our new fore-topmast and main-
topgallant-mast, sprung the main-topmast, and broke
some of the shrouds. It lasted for four hours and then
became calm. Such is the weather close to the Line and
the reason why the crossing is always viewed with appre-
hension. The damage was repaired in three days during
which one of the sailors fell overboard from the maintop.
He would have been drowned—having received a blow on
the head during his fall which rendered him senseless—
had a messmate not immediately leapt overboard, caught
hold of him, and put a rope over his shoulders by which
he was hauled up. The action was brave and showed feeling, for there was danger to be apprehended from sharks
as well as from being pulled under by a drowning man.
Such incidents well show the good-heartedness of the
generality of sailors, something that is often overlooked or
mistaken because of their rough, unpolished manners.

We sailed on through calm, rain, squalls, great heat and
low spirits, until 7 May when, in latitude 2° 1′ north, we
were so fortunate as to meet with the south-east trade.
This wind is just as uncertain as the north-east trade. We
fell in with it much sooner than expected and it stayed
with us as far as latitude 22° 4′ south. On the 9th we
crossed the Line in only moderate heat as the trade was
blowing fresh. There is a forfeit which custom has fixed
upon those who cross the equinox for the first time. It is
taxed at a quart of brandy and a pound of sugar, or half a
crown. Those that are not willing to pay undergo a
christening of some severity. They are hoisted by a rope
tied round their waist to the end of the main yard, and
from thence are given three duckings. We saw all the

ceremony but the ducking, which the captain would not permit to take place for fear of the sharks.

On 21 May, in latitude 20° 35', we caught sight of the island of Trinidad [a small volcanic island in the south Atlantic], seven leagues to the south-west. It is uninhabited, no fresh water having as yet been found on it.

There are two kinds of bird peculiar to this side of the Line, called pintados and albatrosses. The former is very pretty, with black and white feathers regularly marked; the latter is remarkable for the length of its wings, many being six, and some even seven, feet from the tip of one wing to the tip of the other. We have had birds about the ship in all our tracks through this vast ocean, though sometimes several hundred leagues from any known land.

After enduring hard gales, contrary winds and some cold weather, on the 27th of June in latitude 35° 51' south we got soundings with a forty-fathom line off the Cape of Good Hope. As it is dangerous at such a time of year to come near this coast, the wind blowing commonly on it, sailors are satisfied with soundings and compass readings to decide where they are without making land. This was our case, and we doubled the cape at thirty leagues' distance.

As we intended to take what is called the inward passage —that is, between the continent and the island of Madagascar—we proposed to refresh at [St] Augustin bay, but the wind proved so contrary that we did not make the island until 8 July, in latitude 22° 57' south, half a degree to the north of the bay. This obliged us to steer for a river called Morondava on the same island, a great place for the slave trade, and on the morning of the 12th we anchored in nine fathoms of water about three miles out from shore. The land is so very low that the tops of the trees can be seen some time before making the island, which appears at first to be a wood growing out of the sea.

One might imagine, with reason, that after being near five months at sea in a ship so packed with men we would have many sick. But, contrary to former experience, we had such extraordinary fortune in this particular that there were but two men who could be called so; and their disorders they brought from Europe with them.

Our first care on arriving at Morondava was to inform ourselves if we could be supplied with livestock and fresh water. Of the first article we found an abundance—oxen, cows, sheep, goats and fowls in plenty. But the difficulty of watering makes this a bad place to stop at for refreshment. This is occasioned by a sandbank and a prodigious surf which rolls all along this coast and makes it almost impossible either to get a boat in to the watering-place or, when she is laden, to get her off with safety. I and three other officers had like to have been a remarkable example of the dangers in this particular, for never were men nearer drowning. After a two days' excursion on land we were returning to the ship in the evening and, the tide being neap, we struck on the bar. There was a greater surf running than usual and, no sooner had we touched, than the sea washed over us several times and would in all likelihood have overset the boat had it not been for four heavy casks of water that were in her. Had this happened, we would probably all have been drowned, for we were then half a mile from the shore and it was such a terrible sea as few could swim in. The dangers, the noise of the waters, and the night coming on, occasioned a scene of horror, hurry and confusion scarce to be described. But the coxswain, being a clever, knowing fellow, made the sailors leap out of the boat and they thus got her off the bar and turned her towards the beach in order to get ashore as soon as possible. The boat was almost full of water. Just as we arrived, an overgrown sea washed me right out of the boat then, receding, left me dry. I was soon on my feet and far enough inland to be out of reach of any other such breaker. Everyone else got out safe, and thus ended this adventure with the loss of only some few trifles, all of us having stripped in case we had to swim.

These difficulties in traffic with the shore were the reason for our leaving this place as soon as we had brought aboard the quantity of water that was absolutely necessary. We hoped to have our wants supplied abundantly by stopping at an island that lies more to the north-west, called Johanna. With some trouble we got on board five cows and some sheep and fowls, and, on Thursday 1 August, weighed anchor with a fair wind.

In the two days I had ashore at Madagascar, rejoicing to find myself once more on terra firma, I mostly rambled about the country with my gun. The island is very large, computed to be more than a thousand miles in length and three hundred in breadth. It is well watered, fruitful, and abounding with most of the necessaries of life. It is under the government of a number of petty kings who are constantly at war one with the other, by which means they supply themselves with slaves. This is the only traffic carried on with the island, both by Europeans and Moors, who, in exchange, give them fusees, linen, scissors, knives, powder, ball and flints. The part we stopped at is one continuous wood, consisting of tamarind, cocoa, plantain, and a variety of other trees all new to me. The surface of the earth is very fine sand which I suppose does not run deep, else the trees would not thrive as they do. The effects of winter are never seen in these climates, and the woods are constantly green, affording at the same time a pleasing prospect, a cool retreat, and a continual succession of some kind of ripe fruit. The tamarind and a wild plum were the only ones we could find fit to eat, as it was then the middle of the Madagascar winter. The heat, nothing more than agreeable even in the hottest season,

C

is greatly mitigated by a constant sea breeze which begins at twelve noon and lasts until twelve at night.

The riches of Madagascar's inhabitants consist principally of cows and oxen of which they have great plenty, besides herds of wild ones that keep in the inland parts of the country. They differ from ours by a bump that rises between their shoulders, and this is a cut fit for an epicure, being a fine mixture of fat and lean. Partridges there are in abundance, but not equal in taste to ours, and a great variety of other kinds of wildfowl. The bats here are worth taking notice of, having a body and head as large as a fox and wings which, when extended, measure upwards of six feet. The chief nuisance of the island is the alligator. Every river and swamp swarms with them and some are of a monstrous size. Their frequent destruction amongst cattle, and their occasional devouring of a man, bespeak the ravenous, fierce disposition of this animal.

The dwellings of the inhabitants give one reason to conjecture that they are a lazy people. They live in a cabin much resembling ours in Ireland, built of cane and covered with reeds, generally about twelve feet long and ten broad, and surrounded by an area fifty feet square which is fenced and cleared of wood. Their furniture is a mat to lie on and an earthen pot to dress their victuals in. These are all the conveniences that even the captains and great men have. I can impute this great want of all the indulgences of life to no other cause but the frequency of their wars added to the goodness of their climate and countryside, which produces sustenance without any cultivation. As far as I was able to judge, they do not want capacity, being of a very quick and ready comprehension. Both the men and women are extremely well made, and generally of a copper colour. Their features are in no way disagreeable; nay, there was one young girl that almost deserved the name of handsome. Women of the better sort are virtuous, but the slaves are common prostitutes. The dress of the men consists of a piece of linen called by them a *lamber*, about twelve yards long and one broad, which they roll round their waist and at night cover themselves with. Most of them have a gun, powder horn and shot bag, and the rest have spears. The women, besides their *lambers*, have a half-shift which covers their breasts and shoulders. Slaves of both sexes have no other covering than a piece of cloth round their waist. They make a kind of linen of grass, which is very pretty, but most of what they use is brought them by the Moors. Europeans supply them with guns, powder and shot. As to their religion, all I could learn was that they believe in a Great God, who made them, heaven and earth, and who severely punishes a lie; it is a common expression with those that can speak a little English, when they want to convince you of the truth of anything, to assert 'If me lie, God killed me indeed'. They sacrifice, make burnt offerings, and are very superstitious, and the priests give them a thing called an *owly* when they go to war, which they imagine preserves them from the balls and arrows of their enemies. But lest the priestcraft imposition should be found out, they are at the same time taught to believe that God may render the charm ineffectual when it is His will they should be destroyed.

From the whole of the observations which so short a time and the want of knowing their language would permit me to make, I am the more confirmed in an old opinion. That is, that if a person qualified and unprejudiced were to give an account of those people called savages, we should find that the idea we have of those poor creatures—generally nurtured by Europeans to excuse, in some manner, their own cruelties—would prove to be very false and far different from reality. We should find that they have the same faculties as we, most of our virtues and perhaps not so many vices, and that the principal difference is that, in their case, nature wants weeding, whereas in ours, we have spoiled its beauty with too much art.

As I mentioned before, on 1 August we left Madagascar and now reckoned on our voyage being near over, for the winds called monsoons constantly prevail in these seas, blowing from April to September with little variation from the south-west point and the remainder of the year from the north-east. April and October are the months in which they shift, at which time may be expected hurricanes of wind, thunder and lightning. But except those two months it is safe and pleasant sailing in those parts.

We were now in longing expectation of a sight of Johanna, intended as our next stage. It was frequently the subject of our conversation and the captain increased our desire by the charming account he gave of it. He said the inhabitants of the island were a good-natured set of people, and that the place abounded with all manner of fruits, particularly oranges and limes—two articles of the most pleasing to persons who have been long at sea.

On the 5th, at five in the evening, we came in sight of our much-desired island and were within a few miles of the harbour by six the next morning. It appeared a fine country, well varied with mountain and valley, the summit of the highest land being covered with trees. The morning was beautifully fine, the sea calmed to a perfect glass, and the wind just sufficient to fill our sails and smoothly waft us to our much-longed-for port. Thus situated, judge if we were not in spirits. Nay, in the wantonness of our imagination we even smelled the orange and lime trees. Thus we stole on until we saw the bay, at which time clouds began to gather on the hills, the sky lowered, and a sudden and violent squall full off the land obliged us to sheer away. It continued the whole

day to blow and rain and had so little appearance of
clearing up that the captain finally dropped his project
of putting in there, and determined to proceed on his
voyage without stopping. This, to landsmen, must doubtless appear to have been a great disappointment, but we
veterans in sea philosophy, who never rely too much on
appearances, can shift our desires as easily as we do our
sails; and we therefore began to please ourselves with the
thought that we should the sooner arrive at our destined
port.

In the morning, on the 13th, we crossed the Line for the
second time in pleasant weather and with a fresh gale,
and on the 28th came within sight of the island of Ceylon.
This we kept in view until the 31st, sometimes becalmed
and sometimes in squalls, it being remarkable that even
in the most steady time of the monsoon such weather prevails as you approach any of the islands. This is imputed
to the current of air being broken by the high lands which
most of them abound with.

Ceylon is a large island containing a number of mountains. Its principal produce is cinnamon, which can be
smelt very sensibly at three leagues' distance! The Dutch
are masters of all the sea coasts here and have entirely
monopolised the trade. There are several good harbours,
one of the best being Triconamale [Trincomalee], where
English ships frequently go to avoid the bad weather
that commonly occurs on the Coromandel coast at the
shifting of the monsoon.

Our voyage from Madagascar had been very pleasant,
fully answering expectation, the wind constantly fair and
fresh driving us at the rate of 160 miles in the four-and-
twenty hours (as is always the case in the proper season)
except for the little delay we met with off Ceylon. On the
first day of September we saw the land to the southward of
Fort St David and at six in the evening dropped anchor in

the roadstead about three miles from the fort. Shortly
before we anchored, we were surprised with the sight of
a black man who seemed to be walking on the water! On
nearer approach we perceived he was standing on a
couple of beams that were tied together, on which
wonderful vessel, called a cattemoran [catamaran] they
go many leagues to sea even in bad weather. This fellow
had been sent to know our name and from whence we
came.

When we arrived in India, all our men were in better
health than when we embarked, and we had lost none
except the poor soul who fell overboard. Much of this
was, I believe, due to the cleanliness, regularity and
sobriety observed all along as well as to the good provisions which were laid in. The behaviour of Captain
Norway was that of a man of sense, humanity and politeness, and on all occasions he showed himself an extreme
good sailor.

CHAPTER TWO

The morning after our anchoring, I was sent by Lieutenant-Colonel Bagshaw to the governor, to know if we were to land at Fort St David or to proceed to Madras. The fort being fixed on as the place, our detachment was landed on 5 September at a town called Cuddalore, which lies about a mile distant.

The possessions which the East India Company have on this part of the coast consist of a fort and a tract of land round it stretching the length of a cannon-shot in all directions. The original cannon-shot must have been a good one, for the land is very extensive! [In fact, when confronted with this method of drawing a boundary, the Company had sent away for a long-range gun and an expert gunner to use it to best advantage.] It was purchased from the Morattoes [Marathas] for fifty thousand *pagodas* [South Indian coins], upwards of twenty thousand pounds sterling. The fort was at that time nothing but an irregular square fortified according to the Moorish manner, with round towers at the angles. But, contrary to their usual custom, the Company have made the place one of the strongest of their possessions in India, having modernised the fortifications with a good bastion at each angle, a hornwork before the gateway, two half-moons in the ditch—which is wet, and supplied with water—and a well-mined glacis [a sloping bank on the outer perimeter of the ditch or moat]. This has already cost them above twenty thousand pounds more. The fort is but small and well crowded with buildings that would be greatly to its disadvantage if besieged. It is within about half a mile of the sea and commands the country pretty well. Most of the black merchants belonging to the Company reside at the Moorish [Muslim] town of Cuddalore, where we were quartered. This is surrounded with a wall and bastions at proper distances, but has no ditch and would be insufficient and of little service against anything. The town is near two miles in circumference, full of inhabitants and crowded with cabins. A few black merchants have upstair houses. These, and two or three pagodas [*dagobas*, or places of worship] are all the brick buildings in this town. There is generally a small detachment from the fort to garrison the place, but except for these, few other Europeans reside here.

About three miles from this town and one from the fort is one of the neatest pieces of architecture in India, built by one Mr Pitt, deputy governor in the year 1737. He was then carrying on some part of the fortifications and found means at the same time to erect this country house. The apartments and offices are well contrived for the climate and the gardens, parks and avenues all laid out with taste, nothing having been neglected to render it a most commodious, agreeable dwelling. It is situated in a pleasant part of the bounds which are altogether the best-improved piece of land in India, being planted throughout with avenues of fine trees, on a most fruitful spot, diversified with a number of pretty villas built by the gentlemen of the settlement, and all contributing to its embellishment and beauty.

At Fort St David, there are a deputy governor and four councillors, all under the direction of the Council of Madras. He that is appointed deputy is, by the same token, second in Council at Madras. Fort St David has stood them [the Company] in good stead, for at the taking of Madras in the year 1746 it was their only refuge and place of security. Its vicinity to Pondicherry, the French settlement (which is but fifteen miles distant), obliges them to be watchful, as in time of war parties frequently ravage their bounds.

As I have mentioned, on 5 September the detachment from the *Britannia* Indiaman landed at Cuddalore. Colonel Adlercron arrived on the 23rd of the same month. So too did Admiral Watson and part of the fleet, with the greater part of the regiment, all but those who were in the *Cumberland* and *Tyger*.

The situation of the Company's affairs at that time might have given us just reason to expect to be welcome guests; we brought them a reinforcement of 848 land forces besides a considerable fleet. But we were deceived in our expectations, and found that we were both unexpected and unwelcome. Everything was unprovided for our reception and there was no alacrity shown to accommodate us with even what was absolutely necessary in such a climate, much less in that manner which I think we had some reason to expect. Had their [the Company's] situation been more prosperous, their treatment would have been in no way extraordinary, for such is the fate of soldiers—only to be regarded when wanted. But their situation was far otherwise. From whence, then, you may justly ask, could proceed such conduct? Why, from that spirit which has and still continues to prevail amongst their governors and the generality of their servants, that would lead them to prefer to prolong a war that is ruining their trade sooner than receive any assistance from His

Majesty's forces. To welcome us would mean letting us too much into their affairs here, and might give rise to the discovery of things which they do not choose should come to public knowledge. Besides, our officers taking precedence over theirs in their several ranks (a sore thorn in their sides) we should doubtless have the best chance of getting those lucrative commands wherein many have, in a short time, made their fortunes. Thus only can I account for the bad reception we had and the many obstacles which Colonel Adlercron met with in the execution of his power. It seemed to them that the orders the colonel had received from His Majesty clashed with their Charter.

To obviate these difficulties and settle matters, if possible, on a better footing, Lieutenant-Colonel Bagshaw was sent to Madras (the seat of the Presidency) shortly after our arrival. It had not been thought prudent by a council of war that the colonel himself should go. The only result of the mission was the fixing of a most advantageous allowance for His Majesty's troops. A settlement had been made between the colonel and the Directors [in London] of the East India Company before he left England, by which the colonel was allowed forty shillings per day. But the allowance made for the rest of the officers was so little, and so far short of what the Company's officers had, that not one would accept it. The settlement now granted was as follows. The lieutenant-colonel had the value of £46. 17s per month, the major £28. 17s, each captain £10. 17s, the lieutenants, ensigns, chaplain, quartermaster, and surgeon £3. 4s, each surgeon's mate £2 8s, sergeants 13s, corporals 7s 4d, and privates 5s. Besides this, the lieutenant-colonel had five servants, the major four, each captain three, and each subaltern one, at the value each of two pence per day. The same amount went to the captains for each non-effective, and the allowance for every man was always to be paid as if the companies were complete.

This settlement was probably granted in the hope that it would stop complaints and make us rest inactive and quiet. But in order more effectually to render us useless, Mr Saunders—the then governor of Madras—agreed to a suspension of arms which the French readily fell in with; for though they had likewise received some reinforcement from Europe, it was yet far short of what we had. We at that time were much superior. Probably Mr Saunders, who then was determined on returning home to England, desired to take an account of peace home with him, and this may have contributed to patching up matters at a time when we were apparently greatly superior.

But let what will be the cause. On 11 October, the following suspension was published.

ARTICLES concluded between Thomas Saunders Esqr President and Governour on the coast of Coromandel in behalf of the English East India Company; and Charles Robert Godcheu Esqr His most Christian Majesty's commissary, and Governour General of all the French settlements, in behalf of the French East India Company, for a suspension of arms in Karnatec [Carnatic]—

1st To begin from the 11th October, the day on which the suspension of arms shall be published to all the troops, in all the Forts, and actual possessions of the two contracting nations in the Karnatec, all acts of hostility shall cease between the French and English.

2d During the course of this suspension which shall be for three months, their troops shall not act against each other, not only as principals but even as auxiliaries.

3d The two Nations shall oblige their allies to enter into the same agreement.

4th If either of the two nations, French or English, shall commit any act of hostility, possess themselves of any place, or either occasion any damage to the other after the day of the publication of the said suspension, both oblige themselves to make reparation proportionable to the damage and the entire restitution of whatever was taken.

5th If the Allies or others Troops in the pay of either nation, shall commit any act of hostility or plunder the territories of which either nation is now in possession, it shall be lawful for both nations to repulse their insults by force; by which the injured nation shall not be deemed to have infringed the present agreement.

6th If the Allies or Auxiliary troops of either nation shall take arms or insult the Countries of which the nation they were allied to are now in possession, the two nations shall succour each other in this case, to oppose this enemy, who should become thereby a common enemy to both. [i.e. If the territory of either nation should be threatened by a former ally, the other would offer assistance. The implication was that France and England would join together against native powers or, possibly, the Dutch.]

7th The Troops of the two Nations shall be employed during this suspension of arms to secure their settlements and present possessions. They may be freely and without difficulty transported from one place to another at the pleasure of the Governours, Generals, Commanders &c^a of each nation; and all persons actually under the protection of either Flag may in like manner go, and come, without being disturbed either in their effects or persons.

8th There shall be free commerce throughout the Karnatec and in all the countries to the Northward of the Coromandel coast for the two contracting nations;

they may bring goods from all places in the depen-
dencies of either Nation, or their allies, and transport
them freely and without any duty whatever through
their respective territories and Jaqueers [*jagir*:
assigned land].

9th As soon as the suspension of arms is proclaimed, the
mutual exchange of prisoners shall be set about, and
the necessary measures taken in an amicable manner
to soften the fate of those that shall remain; by putting them together into places where they may feel
less the rigour of a long captivity.

Signed in the English copy *Th*^s *Saunders*
in the French copy   *Godeheu*

Before the expiration of the foregoing suspension, a
conditional treaty was settled between the two nations
and a truce concluded to stand until the treaty should be
either approved or rejected by the Directors [in Europe].
Shortly after, Mr Saunders and Mr Godeheu were to sail
for Europe in order to finish there what they had begun
here. They were to be succeeded, the former by Mr Pigot
and the latter by Mr De La Ries.

Until Mr Saunders left the coast, he continued to
thwart Colonel Adlercron in the execution of those
powers which His Majesty had been pleased to give him,
insisting, in particular, that he should have no kind of
command in any of their garrison settlements. This the
lieutenant-colonel seemed to agree with them in. Joined
to this, the necessity of settling a plan of military operations in case of a renewal of the war obliged the colonel at
last to determine on going to Madras. He left Cuddalore
on 4 December 1754, I attending him as his secretary, to
which office I had been appointed on the colonel's arrival
on the coast.

The method of travelling in this country differs much

from that in Europe, Eastern luxury having invented a
vehicle the most easy and indulgent that could possibly
be thought of. It is a kind of portable bed, called palanquin, that is suspended on a bamboo and carried on men's
shoulders. Eight men are commonly the number requisite
for a journey, five under it at one time, who are relieved
turn about. These fellows will go at the rate of five miles
an hour with great ease and hold it for many days. As for
utensils, provisions, and servants to dress [cook] them, it
must be the traveller's care to provide all, as nothing is to
be had on the roads but house-room in places which are
called *choultries*, built by private persons for the use of the
public. These are to be found in great numbers all over
this country. I shall take more particular notice of them
hereafter. One of these houses is generally your shelter at
night. Here you make your fire, dress your supper, and
find a good bed in your palanquin.

Thus equipped we set out for Madras. The first place
of any note on the road belongs to the French. It is called
Arian-Coapang. It is a small square fort with a good, wet
ditch, about ten miles north of Fort St David. I mention
it not because it is anything remarkable in itself, but because it once provided a demonstration of how very little
the British were acquainted with the situation of a place
belonging to an enemy and only a few miles from our
bounds. When Mr [Admiral] Boscawen laid siege to Pondicherry in the year 1748, Arian-Coapang was thought to be
only a house surrounded with a wall. The grenadiers of his
force were ordered to attack it and paid severely for their
ignorance, a great number of them being killed as they
marched round it without being able to annoy the enemy
in the least.

In the morning of the 5th, we arrived at Pondicherry,
which is about fifteen miles north of Fort St David. This
is the capital of the French settlements in the East Indies.

Mr Godeheu, who succeeded Mr Dupleix, was governor at that time and received the colonel with great politeness. His habitation was a palace that had been begun by a former governor, called Le Noir; but the succeeding governor, Mr Dumas, finding the expense too great, put a stop to the work just after the foundations were raised. When Mr Dupleix came to the government, his fondness for magnificence and the immense quantity of wealth which he found means to accumulate induced him to complete this beautiful palace, where grandeur of building and elegance of furniture join to form an habitation suitable for a king. Its situation takes away greatly from the beauty of its appearance, for, being built within the citadel, it is on all sides confined and therefore wants that area which such a piece of architecture deserves to show it to greatest advantage.

The town appeared to be of great extent, surrounded with a wall and bastions, and well inhabited, particularly by blacks—which will always be the case in this country, as it is the only security they can have against the frequent incursions of the Morattoes, a banditto kind of soldier [troops of the native Maratha confederacy]. There are handsome brick houses, and an extensive open piazza near the sea gate supported by pillars that were brought from Madras when it was taken by the French. The town is situated close to the sea, which is commanded by a strong battery. But nature has secured this part with a great surf which makes it very dangerous to land in any other boats than those belonging to the country, which are built purposely for it. The boatmen are by frequent practice very dexterous, yet accidents sometimes happen. This surf prevails all along the coast of Coromandel.

On the 7th, we arrived at a Dutch settlement called Sadras, where they have a square fort regularly fortified. In it live the governor and principal factors [merchants] of the place. The Black Town is small and partakes somewhat of that neatness which is particular to the European colony.

On the 8th we came to a Moorish town called Tripaloor, where a pagoda was being built and I had the opportunity of observing a particular method of raising stones up to the top of the walls. As they build, they pile up earth which, as the building rises, grows to a mound. Up this they drag stones of extraordinary size. When the building is finished, they scoop the earth out of the inside and at the same time cut it off the outside.

There is in this town a fine reservoir of water (called, in the country language, tank), three hundred feet square, with a good parapet wall round it and steps the whole length of each side down to the water's edge. Such things abound all over the country, particularly near their places of worship. As cleanliness is absolutely necessary in these climates, they have prudently made frequent washing one of the articles of their religion.

On the 9th, we passed by St Thomas, a settlement which used to belong to the Portuguese, situated three miles from Madras. The English, finding the neighbourhood of the Portuguese not so conformable to their interest as they could wish, have taken it into their own possession. Thus contemptible have now become those first discoverers and one-time masters of all the coast of India. They have left an eternal monument in the universal use of their language all over these parts. In this place, the English have a trifling fort with a ditch round it. The ruins here show it to have been once as considerable as it is now miserly and beggarly. The same day we arrived at Madras, where the Colonel was saluted at entrance with thirteen guns.

The country through which we passed, though close to the sea, appears capable of producing everything for the

use, and even convenience, of life. But it is so thinly inhabited, and consequently little cultivated, that it is not
much better than in a state of nature. The causes assigned
are the troubles that have continued for some years past,
which, subjecting the poor inhabitants to frequent
plundering by the Marathas, oblige them to fly to the
towns for protection.

The settlement at Madras is the principal one belonging
to the English on the coast of Coromandel, and to it all
the others in that part of India are subject. It has a government and eight or ten gentlemen called councillors, who
form a board and transact all mercantile affairs by
majority decision. Besides this, there is a committee (of
which the governor is always president) appointed by the
Directors whose particular province is settling all military
operations and everything relative to negotiations with
the country [native] powers. What lies in their province is
done without any of the councillors—except those on the
committee—being acquainted with it.

The situation of Madras is reckoned very bad for a
trading colony. It has no security for ships and a roadstead wild and open, besides a most dangerous surf which
makes the landing difficult and dangerous. There are two
towns, the European and the Black towns. The former is
well built, with lofty houses and flat roofs, but the streets
are very narrow except for those immediately about the
governor's habitation, which is in the middle and was the
first building the English made after they landed. It consists of a tolerably good house surrounded with offices
and a slight wall, and is properly called Fort St George.
The Capuchins had a fine church in this town which was
demolished three years ago on an order from the Court of
Directors in London. Part of the outbuildings still remain
and serve for officers' barracks.

Great alterations have been made in the fortifications

D

since our arrival. Before, the principal strength consisted in a fine glacis—made by the French when in possession of it—at the north and south ends. A plan, made by Mr Robins, had been begun some years ago but discontinued. On the present war with the French, however, they renewed the work with such spirit and despatch as has now rendered it one of the strongest places in India. There are several excellent good bastions, and a broad, deep, wet ditch. All the adjacent country is commanded from the batteries except a small hill at the north-west end which, if they continue as they have begun, will soon be carried away and serve to make the glacis. The town is not only strengthened but considerably enlarged by these works.

The Black Town was formerly close to the fort, but the French destroyed a good part in order to make an esplanade. The new works, extending still further that way, have obliged them to demolish more, notwithstanding which it is of a considerable extent. The houses here, according to the custom of the country, are low and make a very poor appearance. The Black Town used to be surrounded by a wall which the French demolished, and it now remains entirely open. A considerable trade was formerly carried on here, but the little security the black merchants were afforded by the English when the French besieged the place induced many of them to repair to Pondicherry. This, joined to the long continuance of the war, has reduced it now to a very inconsiderable state, all kinds of manufactures being scarce and not so good as formerly.

About seven miles to the westward of this town is a place called the Mount, where most of the European gentlemen retire to at this season of the year, it being their spring. There are here a number of pretty villas situated at the foot of a hill covered with loose, cragged, stony shrub and trees. On the summit is a Portuguese church with 133 steps, and there are proper resting points or landings from the bottom to the top of the Mount. Altogether it affords a pleasing, rural appearance, particularly in this part of the country which is mostly flat. A mile before you come to it is a place called the 'little Mount' where, superstitious tradition says, lived St Thomas [the Apostle]. Here is the very cave he inhabited, a fountain that miraculously sprang up at his command, the mark of his hand on a rock occasioned by his falling down when pursued by his destroyers. In short, every spot of this hill bears some record of its inhabitant. The most rational account I have heard of the rise of this tradition is that a Syrian merchant called Mar Thoma settled on this coast and, being a Christian, introduced that belief in these parts. They have now added to the absurdities of the church of Rome most of the pagan ceremonies, and have made a religion that appears much more ridiculous than that professed by the original inhabitants. At present, there is an Armenian church built over the cave, in the front of which is a stone that had an inscription on it of which nothing is now legible but the date 1612.

Near this place is a bridge called Marmelong, built over a river of the same name that is little more than a rivulet in the dry season but of great extent in the rains. The bridge consists of twenty-nine arches, each about twenty feet diameter and two smaller ones at each end of ten feet. Its length is 1100 feet and its breadth thirty-two at the entrance of the battlements, gradually lessening to ten in the centre. There are two large pillars at each end, and on one is the following inscription:

HUNC PONTEM EDIFICARI IUSSIT PRO BONO PUBLICO

COIA PETRUS USCAN NATIONE ARMENI

ANNO SALUTIS MDCCXXVI

This bridge and the steps up the Mount were built by the same person, who left—to keep them in repair—twenty thousand *pagodas*, about eight thousand pounds of our money.

But to return to the occasion of our journey. The colonel, on his arrival at Madras, found the gentlemen of the committee apparently in better disposition than he expected. Mr Saunders was a man of reputedly great knowledge concerning the Company's interest and affairs in India, who did most of the business himself. Not being of a disposition fond of gaiety or that state and parade which, by persons of his rank, is generally much affected in these parts, he was therefore little disturbed from the close application in which he seemed to take pleasure. He was of a cunning turn, not talkative, seldom speaking but with design, and he had a particular talent for finding out a man's favourite passion to which he would artfully and insensibly lead the conversation, thereby gaining a kind of confidence that laid one more open to his purposes. Such was the person who particularly acted in this affair and in a short time seemingly settled matters with the colonel to the satisfaction of both parties. Then, treating it as a thing of no great consequence, through the mean drift of his reconciling disposition he persuaded the colonel to take back all the public letters he had written— containing mostly complaints against Mr Saunders and the Council—and write others conformable to the present situation of affairs. This was accordingly done.

On 20 December there arrived His Majesty's ships *Cumberland* and *Tyger* with the remainder of the regiment, and shortly after the *Tyger* was despatched with them to join the main body at Fort St David.

The colonel now having finished the business that had called him to Madras, and having received from the committee a plan of military operations in case it should be found necessary to commence hostilities again, now decided to return to the regiment. Accordingly we set out on 24 December and arrived at Cuddalore on the 27th. As this place was thought to contribute somewhat to the mortality with which we were then much afflicted, the colonel applied to be removed. His application was granted and the garden house I have mentioned was appointed as our quarters. We repaired there on 13 January 1755.

Mr Saunders sailed for Europe some time in January and was succeeded by Mr Pigot, who had been chief of a small settlement on the same coast, called Vizagapatam. He was a man of a very different disposition from the former. Easy, genteel in his address, and fond of pleasure, he had made himself agreeable to the colonel at Madras. This promised a continuance of the good disposition matters then were in, but shortly it proved otherwise and the old discontent began to renew with as great animosity as ever. Indeed, the colonel's orders and the Company's Charter so clashed together as to render it almost impossible, unless one side or the other relinquished something of what they thought their right, for harmony to subsist long between them. It now appeared that Mr Saunders had outwitted the colonel in persuading him to recall his former complaints. Mr Saunders believed that he would be home in England before new complaints arose and could there guard against their consequences. In order to repair what was done, the colonel sent a full and ample narrative of all grievances to Europe the October following.

Since signing the conditional treaty, the English Company had employed their troops in collecting the rents due to the Nabob [of Arcot] in the Madura and Tinnevelly countries. The chiefs in these places had taken advantage of the commotions in the state by refusing during all the troubles to account for the revenues of their several districts. The command was given to Lieutenant-Colonel Heron, a gentleman that had held that rank in His Majesty's service, but had lately come out from England with the rank of major in the Company's service. He marched with the army to the country concerned but fulfilled the intentions of the Company so badly that they recalled him and brought him to court martial for the following crimes.

The first General Charge was: For perverting the intention of his commission. In that contrary to the intent and meaning of his instructions, instead of collecting the revenues of Madura and Tinnevelly, Lieutenant-Colonel Heron did of his own assumed authority farm out those revenues to Manphoos Cawn [Manfuz Khan], an officer of the Nabob's, with whom Colonel Heron ought to have acted in conjunction for the joint interest of the Nabob and Company and not have entered into self-interested and private contracts.

A second instance laid against him of the above charge was that he applied to his own use, and that of other private persons, or that he suffered to be so applied, sums of money which were collected from the Pollygars [poligar: feudal chief] and ought to have been brought to the Company's account.

A second General Charge was that he laid, or for his own private advantage authorised, a duty on the necessaries of life brought into garrison.

A third General Charge was breach of orders, and a fourth and last General Charge was of behaving in a manner unbecoming an officer.

He was found guilty of the first and last charges and thereby rendered incapable of further service. After having punished him by martial law, they desired to attack him also by civil law, but he, hearing of their intention, fled to

Pondicherry and from thence returned to Europe. As I consider courts martial to be tribunals of great justice, so I cannot but look on Colonel Heron as guilty, and I am confirmed in that opinion by the fact that the gentleman in the space of a few months found means to accumulate about twelve thousand pounds. It may be said, and it has been said by many, that as in most points he acted only in a manner agreeable to custom his sentence was rather severe. But can that general ruling power [custom] subvert the more ancient one of justice and make the fault less? He who has not a better standard for his actions is little to be depended on. Indeed, it seems too much the principle established by men in these parts and I cannot help taking notice that, as far as has fallen under my observation, the Company in general are but indifferently served, though some individuals are men of the greatest worth.

When Colonel Heron quitted the army, the command devolved on Captain Pollier. He was to escort the Nabob to Madras. On his way thither, the Nabob took the opportunity of calling at Fort St David to see Admiral Watson and Colonel Adlercron. The first visit was paid by the colonel, on 31 July 1755, and returned on 5 August. The Nabob was attended by a multitude of people, a number of elephants, camels and horsemen, altogether making a grand appearance. The regiment was drawn up in two lines from the garden house gate as far as they could extend. When the Nabob first entered the lines, he got off his elephant and walked through the ranks, a march beating, colours lowered, and officers saluting—which he returned to each with a dignity and grace becoming a prince. After a short visit, the regiment was formed and went through their firings and evolutions, seemingly much to his satisfaction. He had that morning been on board the admiral's ship and was greatly surprised at its size and number of guns. Yet novelty seems, in general, to move Indians but in a small degree, and neither by actions nor words do they show much emotion even at things which certainly ought to be extraordinary to them. The observations they make on such occasions are commonly puerile, manifesting either a natural insensibility or weak judgement.

Mahomet Allee Cawn [Muhammad Ali Khan], the present nabob, is a comely, handsome man of princely deportment, with a goodness in his aspect that speaks much in his favour. Since his appointment to the nabob-ship, it has been one continued scene of trouble and danger, which he has supported with great firmness and resolution of mind. He was very rich at his father's death, but the great expense of supporting his title has long since not only exhausted all his ready money but likewise run him in debt so much with the Company as to oblige him to mortgage the greatest part of his dominions, reducing himself almost to what they please to allow him—which at times has been so far from sufficient to maintain his dignity that it barely suffices to provide the necessaries for life for him and his family.

CHAPTER THREE

Affairs on the coast were in this situation when I resigned
my secretaryship to Colonel Adlercron. The confinement
of this employment had not only much impaired my health
but had likewise prevented me going to my friend Caillaud
(who then commanded at Trichinopoly, a place about
two hundred miles to the south-west of Fort St David).
The obstacle to my desired visit being removed, I was
able to accept the many pressing invitations I had had
and left the garden house on 28 November 1755.

The place that first deserves note on the road to
Trichinopoly is called Chillingbrum [Chidamburam],
which is about thirty miles from Fort St David and has a
considerable pagoda [in honour of Siva]. It was formerly
held in a great degree of veneration by the natives but
fell, in the late troubles, first into the hands of the English
and later into those of the French. It being a place of
some strength and of great service in keeping a free
passage open into the country, they by avarice, curiosity
and necessity have entered into the most secret parts of
the temple and have thus—according to the superstitious

notion of these poor natives—so much polluted it that the temple now begins to be entirely abandoned.

The temple consists of several detached buildings, all surrounded with two walls about forty yards distant from each other, high and strong, built in a square form to enclose the whole. Each face has an entrance or gateway over which is erected a kind of pyramidical building, generally about seven storeys in height. The exterior sides are crowded with a heap of rude, indecent figures that, from the similitude they bear to what I have observed on all buildings of that kind, induces me to imagine they are representations of some fabulous traditions concerning their gods. The enclosed area is full of a variety of temples, some large, some small, containing their different divinities, beside which is a large basin surrounded with a handsome piazza. The inside appears not to have ever been finished, yet what is accomplished shows the labour of an infinite number of hands and altogether has something of grandeur, proceeding not from any taste in the architecture but from the magnitude of the building, stones of a prodigious size being raised a considerable height. I had an opportunity of particularly observing this, as the result of an accident which had happened a few days before my arrival; a thunder clap had cloven one of the pyramidical buildings and disclosed very large stones almost at its summit.

The insides of these temples are gloomy and dark, impressing a kind of horror on the mind of the beholder. At the further end is placed the image, the object of their worship, elevated from the level of the ground by four or five steps where none but the priests are allowed to approach. Thus, by dread and respect, the vulgar are kept in that submission to their imaginary divinities which prevents the free use of their reason—which soon would unveil the roguery and lies of their Bramines [*Brahmin*: the priestly caste]. But priestcraft here, as well as in some more enlightened countries, knows well how to make use of vulgar, erroneous tradition to blind the rational faculties which are always weakest where traditions are most numerous. Strange and absurd as this worship is, yet would it be difficult to alter it, for such is the tenacious attachment and respect of these people for the opinions and customs of their forefathers that they cannot be persuaded to alter in even the most trifling things. Nor have they any books to assist them in shaking off superstition, which, being contracted in infancy and gaining strength as they grow older, becomes a second nature. The figures they worship are likewise formed to raise terror and fear, being mostly of an uncouth and horrid aspect, some half beast, half man, with elephants' and serpents' heads. One I particularly observed was a colossean figure, the upper part of which represented a man with fourteen hands, in each of which was some emblematical figure. The pedestal and figure—upwards of eight feet in height, six in length and five in breadth—were all cut out of one stone. In the temple which contains this figure is the remains of a remarkable stone chain, five links of which are still entire, hanging by a stone ring from a pillar upwards of twenty feet high, all one stone. The links are quite separate, one from the other, and, according to the tradition of the place, extended to another pillar ten feet distant. There is an unfinished temple here consisting of upwards of three hundred pillars, many of which are near twenty feet high, each from one stone.

The pyramidical buildings over the gateways are mostly made of brick, excellent for colour and hardness, and the cement is extraordinarily good. On the whole, it is a most curious temple which only a close inspection lasting some days would enable one person to give a particular account of.

I left this place on the 29th at about five o'clock in the morning. I crossed a river called the old Coleroon at about seven, it being then fordable. It has acquired the epithet of 'old' because a considerable flood resulted in the formation of a new bed, which I crossed shortly after in a boat, it being deep and rapid. The town of Chially where I arrived half an hour after twelve, is of great extent but with the exception of some pagodas its buildings are mean, all on the same model, and differing only in size. In the town are likewise several *choultries*, which are generally nothing more than a square piazza open only on one side. They are, as I said before, built for the convenience of travellers and are all the accommodation to be met with on these roads. At every hour's distance one sees such shelters, some better than others, and erected by private persons. They are always near water and where rice may be had. Building one is looked upon as a great act of charity, which doubtless it is, and it must principally proceed from public spirit. Yet there seems to be something of vanity thus to hand down a name to posterity, for these buildings are called after him that erected them. And a son, sooner than repair a *choultry* built by his father, will raise another on purpose to give it his own name. Thus they soon run to ruin. But let the motive be what it will, the utility is general, affording all over this part of the country a very good shelter from the inclemency of the weather.

Nothing worth observation occurred on the road until the 30th, in the morning, when I arrived at a town called Miaverum. Here is the most remarkable *choultry* in this country; it consists of a square building open in the centre. The face that fronts the main street of the town has a very handsome gateway, much ornamented with figures according to the custom of the country, which makes a tolerably grand appearance. By this, you enter into a square surrounded with a piazza. The parts on the right and left are ninety-seven paces in length and nine in depth, and have two rows of pillars open only on the inside and elevated from the level of the ground about ten feet. The piazza in the front is open through, is forty-nine paces long and consists of forty square pillars in four rows of ten lengthwise. Each end is terminated by a wing fourteen paces long, projecting ten paces from the level of the front. Close to this face runs the river Coleroon, and there is a descent of sixteen steps, with four landing-places, continued the whole length of the front. This gives a great air of grandeur to the building. In the inside of the square is a kind of cupola supported by twelve pillars and raised nine steps high. There is also a handsome parapet round the top of the whole building and the inside is painted with a great variety of symbolic figures and ornaments. Yellow and red are the two prevailing colours, which, though gaudy, have no unpleasing effect on the beholder. The town is esteemed by the Gentoos, the name given to the original inhabitants of this country [from the Portuguese word for heathen or 'gentile'; used to refer to Hindus as distinct from Muslims or Moors], as a very holy place. It is further remarkable for handsome dancing girls (women kept on purpose to dance, and sing, before their gods). I saw some which did not belie report.

Monday, 1 December, I arrived about eleven in the morning at Comboconum [Kumbakonam], a very large, extensive town full of pagodas and *choultries*. One of the former is remarkable for being the highest in this country, consisting of eleven storeys. There is also a tank (reservoir of water) where a miracle is performed every twelve years. To see it, the king of this country (Tanjore) and all considerable persons for many miles about resort to this town, leaving behind them a voluntary tribute as a reward for the priestcraft's imposition. On a particular day of the twelfth year, the tank is agitated by divine influence and there rises from the bottom a flower and a lime. At that signal, the multitude watching for it plunge into the water and are thereby purified of their sins. So prodigious, generally, are the numbers that attend on this occasion and so precipitately do they rush in, that if the tank were not near emptied that day many would in all likelihood be drowned.

About three in the afternoon of the next day, I arrived at Tricatapoly, where there is a strong mud fort garrisoned by the king of Tanjore's soldiers, this being one of his frontier towns. The country through which I had hitherto passed belongs to the forementioned king, and is as pleasing to the eye as any I ever saw. Most all the road has the appearance of an avenue, being bordered on each side with the beautiful Bannion [banyan] tree. There are extensive plains, usually full of rice, interspersed with many clumps of trees and an abundance of little rural villages. In other parts there is pastureland full of fine cattle which this country is remarkable for. Another great attraction is the variety of greens which the rice affords, from the most beautiful springing green through many shades to rich russet. In fine, nothing is wanting to produce the finest landscape but hills. The constant uniformity of a beautiful plain fatigues the eyes of the beholder who wants a rising ground, as it were, to rest the wearied sight upon. Yet wisely is it ordered otherwise, for as nothing is produced here but by the agency of water, high lands—which probably would be destitute of that useful element—would be horrid and barren. As the country has been but little afflicted by the calamities of the late wars, it retains its native beauty, which justly gives a stranger a most charming idea of these parts.

The 3rd of December, about twelve in the morning, I came to Trichinopoly, to the mutual satisfaction of two friends. This town used to be one of the most considerable belonging to the Gentoo government and was formerly the residence of one of their kings. It still retains visible marks of its ancient splendour and opulence, for throughout the whole are remains of stately and grand buildings in the style of architecture of the country, which somewhat resembles the Gothic. Its circumference is about four miles and it is defended by two walls and a good ditch. The inward wall has a rampart which, at the bottom, is about thirty feet in breadth and lessens as it rises in the form of steps to about six feet at the top. There are high battlements and round towers at proper distances. The gateways, which are four in number, are remarkably well defended. It is situated on a fine plain with a natural glacis all round it and no ground that could, in the least, be said to command it. Since the English have had the town in their possession they have built some bastions which have not a little increased its strength.

In the centre of Trichinopoly there is a large rock near a mile in circumference and about four hundred feet high. On the south side of the rock are built one large and several small pagodas and many *choultries*, and there are stairs from the bottom to the top, in number 335. The whole is very stupendous and a work of infinite labour. At the summit is a *choultry* which commands a most extensive, beautiful prospect. There are, besides this, all over the town several very fine and large *choultries* and a most capacious palace which was the former habitation of the kings. It consisted of some hundreds of apartments, several small and large courts, and a garden, but it has now fallen to ruin. In this, as in all other towns, are reservoirs of water, or tanks, but there is one in particular which is remarkably large. It abounds with alligators, some of a monstrous size, which the natives hold in a great degree of veneration and never molest or destroy.

The circumference which the town now occupies was built at three different times. At first it was nothing more than a wall round the rock. Then as the inhabitants increased—they being fond of living within walls which provide their only security against the frequent incursions of the Marathas—this area became too small and it had to be extended. There are still the remains of very considerable houses which show it to have been a handsome, grand and populous city. It is now in the hands of the English in trust for the Nabob, and here they keep a considerable garrison as it is a possession of great consequence in this part of the country. This is particularly so as the French have a town just opposite at about two miles' distance. It is called Syrringham [Seringam] and is separated from Trichinopoly by the river Coleroon.

Seringam is esteemed as a place of the greatest sanctity. It forms a square surrounded with seven walls. In the centre is the pagoda where none but the priests reside. Between the enclosures of each wall, which measure about three hundred feet, live the inhabitants and the French. The latter, though masters of the place, have never yet got beyond the third wall, the natives looking on any place where a Christian treads as polluted. Were the French, by any act of force, to break through this prejudice, it would be of bad consequence to their interests as this temple is held in the greatest degree of veneration and a general revolt would doubtless be occasioned by any threat to its purity. Each of the seven walls has four gateways. One is very remarkable for its beauty and magnitude, being the handsomest piece of Eastern architecture in these parts. It is somewhat of the Gothic taste, yet grand and pleasing to behold. But what is very extraordinary is the prodigious size of some of the stones employed in this building. There are four which, as pillars, support the top and measure in the shaft thirty-two feet

besides the capital. Each is an entire stone. Still more surprising are those that are laid across the top of this gateway; they measure thirty-three feet ten inches in length
and are five and a half feet thick one way and four feet
ten inches the other. Carrying these from the quarry and
then raising them would be a hard task even for Europeans
to accomplish, requiring all their knowledge of mechan-
ism to effect. But here, where they are entirely destitute
of that assistance, it makes it much more worthy of notice.
This can have been accomplished by no other means
than that I have mentioned before, of filling with earth
as they build and then dragging up those ponderous
weights by a multitude of hands. This gateway, which is
in the outward wall facing Trichinopoly, was never
finished, yet what is, is well worth the inspection of the
curious.

The road from Trichinopoly to Seringam has the remains of several very handsome *choultries*; in particular,
along the river side, there is a range of them upwards of
half a mile in length. But these, as most of the public
buildings, are now falling to ruin. The period of this
general desolation can be fixed as beginning when the
Moors first invaded and conquered the country, they being
a set of indolent, lazy people no way inclined to any of the
arts or sciences. Since that time, the Gentoo spirit seems
broke and all those monuments of their opulence are now
running to decay. If any remains of public spirit still
break out in putting up this kind of building, they are
small and trifling in comparison with those of former
times. Also, the war fomented by the English and the
French has greatly contributed to the desolate appearance
of some parts of the country at present. However, notwithstanding the ravages suffered by buildings and plantations—which abound hereabout—natural fruitfulness
could not be harmed and, when I was there, two years of

E

peace had partly restored the beauty of this country, and its air of plenty.

In such surroundings, I passed my time with all the happiness that the society of a valued friend can afford until, on 10 February 1756, the probability of the French raising some disturbance in the country led to my being summoned to quarters. I received the letter in the morning and set out a few hours after with all that could make my journey expeditious.

As I have already told of everything I thought worthy of note on this road, I shall only mention the despatch with which one may travel in a palanquin. I left Trichinopoly, with ten men to carry me, on the 10th at about five in the evening, and arrived at Fort St David in the morning of the 14th. In this time I travelled forty-two hours, about ten each day. Allowing but five miles an hour—a computation rather under than over—this makes 210 miles, a distance that in Europe would be great to accomplish in somewhat less than four days, even on horseback. During this travelling time, too, I was often obliged to hold back for those persons who carried my provisions and baggage, for, though their burdens were light, they could not keep up.

On my return to quarters, I found this sudden summons had been occasioned by a Killidare [*killadar*] or governor of a fort called Vallour [Vellore], who had always been tributary to our Nabob [of Arcot]. Because of the late troubles he had run some years in arrears and now refused to pay; in this, according to report, he was supported by the French who it was thought might take the field in his defence. The Nabob applied to the English for assistance in bringing this governor to reason, and Major Kilpatrick (a gentleman of great worth belonging to the Company's service) was sent against him with about four hundred Europeans who, it was thought, would be sufficient if the

French stood neuter. If they did not, our regiment was then to take the field. As the French did not stir in this affair, it was soon made up and all was quiet again.

As there is not one harbour on the extensive coast of Coromandel, all ships are obliged to leave it at the shifting of the monsoons, in April and October. Admiral Watson and the fleet had, on that account, in October last gone to Bombay, a considerable settlement which the Company have on the Malabar coast. The design was then formed of destroying Angria, a noted pirate in those parts. For many years he had lived unmolested in his principal fort of Geriah; one of our admirals, Mr Mathews, had even miscarried in an attempt to take it. This year there had arrived from Europe a considerable reinforcement of the king's artillery; and Colonel Clive, a gentleman whose character will be greatly exemplified in the following sheets. With this addition to their forces and the assistance of the Marathas—with whom Angria (though one himself) had long been at variance—the siege of Geriah was undertaken. Angria, terrified at this powerful armament, imprudently left the defence of his fort to one of his generals and fled to the Marathas to try and dissuade them from continuing the alliance which would lead to his ruin. It was to no purpose, for they kept him prisoner. In the meantime the fort was attacked both by sea and land, the former forces commanded by Admiral Watson and the latter by Colonel Clive. It was taken after a two days' siege, mainly as a result of fright rather than through any damage done to the walls. These were built of such hard stone as to receive scarce any impression from the shot, and, according to the gentlemen of the squadron, had it been but tolerably defended it would have baffled a much more considerable force. The English lost but thirteen men in this action and few wounded.

There was found in the place money to the value of

about £100,000 in bullion and coin, besides valuable
effects, and many ships in the harbour of considerable
force, called *grabs* [Arab galleys], that were all burnt.
Angria's wives and children were all taken prisoner.

The Marathas had been induced to lend their assistance
by a promise that, if the place was taken, it would be
delivered into their hands. When it was taken, however,
the English refused to fulfil the promise until the will of
the Directors in London was known. But this breach of
the promise exasperated the Marathas to such a degree
as to threaten to draw that powerful enemy on England's
back, and the Company was obliged, through fear, to
do what in justice they ought to have done at first. By
all accounts, transferring Geriah from Angria to the
Marathas has only changed the ownership without re-
moving the evil; the present possessors are proceeding on
the same principles as Angria did.

After this success, the fleet returned to Fort St David on
14 May 1756 and along with it Colonel Clive, who was
appointed deputy governor and to succeed to the presidency. At this time we had a strong rumour of the war
with France in Europe and, the fleet being but thinly
manned because of sickness, Admiral Watson applied to
Colonel Adlercron for some part of the regiment to supply
the deficiency on board each ship. As this was conformable with the orders the colonel had received from His
Majesty, a detachment of 280 men was appointed for that
duty, including other officers and myself. We embarked
on 13 June 1756.

In the road of Fort St David we remained about five
weeks, until the presidency, thinking it more useful to the
Company to have the regiment at their principal settlement, applied for that purpose to the admiral and
colonel. The whole was therefore embarked and, on 20
July, the fleet sailed for Madras, arriving the same day.

Here the regiment landed, except for the detachment that had been first sent on board to man the ships.

As my duty shortly after this obliged me to leave the coast of Coromandel, I will take this period to give an account of some observations I made on the country, customs and manners of the people.

CHAPTER FOUR

Man's mind naturally, from reading and verbal accounts, forms notions of places and things, but such ideas ought not to be depended upon, being often erroneous either through the misrepresentations of the author or prejudice of the reader, generally contracted from a very limited view of things. At least so it was with me. The idea I had of this part of the world I found to be very different from reality. I expected nothing but a scorching sun, a parched country inhabited by a set of savage idolaters, sickness and death in abundance, and life gloomy, sad and melancholy. On experience the phantom vanished and I was agreeably disappointed, for bountiful nature has not here been sparing of her blessings.

The climate in my opinion is very fine, the months of January, February and March being most delightfully pleasant and the heats tempered all day long by cooling sea breezes. The earth is covered with new verdure occasioned by the preceding rains which not only greatly contribute to mitigate the power of a perpendicular sun but refresh and embellish nature with all the charms of a cheerful spring. April is hot for three or four hours before and after midday but the ground is frequently watered with plenteous showers as, in this month, there comes what is called the little monsoon. This is the time when those periodical winds which constantly prevail in these seas shift. From the north-east point they blow six months in the year, and from the south-west the other six. But their influence does not extend to the shore. The time when they change is generally attended with rain, wind, thunder and lightning. The April change is short and seldom as violent as that in October.

May, June, July, August and September are much the hottest in the year, the cooling sea breeze sometimes not blowing for as much as seven days. In lieu of the sea breeze then there is a scorching land wind that commonly comes from the north-west, so violent that it smothers with sand and parches with heat. But this providentially seldom happens. In October the north-east monsoon sets in, which is more or less always ushered in by a storm. The rains then begin and continue until the middle of December, in which space of time falls most of the water that is to serve the people for the ensuing year. For this purpose it is kept in large reservoirs or tanks and issued out as necessity requires for the different uses of their culture. Much is wanted but they are well supplied, the rains being exceeding heavy and sometimes continuing for two or three days with little intermission.

The country then affords a new and pleasing scene, being one continuous sheet of water interspersed with little groves, houses and green islands. When the rains are extraordinarily violent (as was the case in October 1754) they do great damage, frequently sweeping away whole villages and herds of cattle. One of the greatest plagues attending this season is the quantity and variety of insects and vermin, which are driven into the houses.

Mosquitoes, snakes, scorpions, rats, mice, frogs are our constant guests and make the blessing attending St Patrick's land, in this particular, sensibly felt by us his children.

This monsoon is not always as violent. When there has been a deficiency, provident nature sends frequent showers in the months of July, August and September to remedy it. For on this useful element depends plenty or scarcity. There is one thing very remarkable, that heavy dews seldom fall in the fine season of the year, and even when they do they are in no way pernicious. Most of our men, after the example of the Company soldiers, lay out in the open air, free from all shelter, without the least bad consequence attending it. Surely where the exhalations are so free from anything malignant, there the climate must be healthy!

After the rains have ceased, the country shows to the greatest advantage as the rice, which is the natives' principal grain, grows then almost at sight and soon covers the earth with a charming green. The soil is generally sandy, yet so well adapted to the climate as to yield two, and in some places three, crops in the year. But this is not without the assistance of art, which principally consists in refreshing the ground during the dry season with a daily supply of water. Those parts which the tanks cannot supply are nevertheless furnished at a small expense and little trouble, for nature has so ordained it that wherever you dig water is found at nine or ten feet below surface. It is conveyed to the field by the aid of a most simple machine which is nothing more than two trunks of trees, one fixed in the ground perpendicularly and the other balanced on top of it. At one end of the latter is hung a kind of bucket that holds near a third of a barrel, and at the other end is a weighty stone to help raise the water more easily. On the horizontal trunk are a couple of men who work this machine by moving towards the bucket end to sink it in the well and towards the other end to raise it. There is likewise a man at the mouth of the well to turn it out. And these three persons, at the expense of twopence-halfpenny each per day, will water six or more acres by laying them about four inches under water. The growth of rice is very particular. It is first sown in a small piece of ground as thickly as possible. When about six inches up from the ground, it is taken and transplanted into larger fields, five or six stalks together, the little clumps being set about seven inches asunder. The fields are then covered with water and kept so until the rice comes to maturity. There are several other kinds of corn that do not require so much moisture and spread a pleasing verdure on rising grounds that otherwise would look barren and dismal.

As to the instruments made use of in their culture, I verily believe they are the model of the first invented, without the least improvement or addition. This is not, I think, owing to any want of genius in the people, but to a most tenacious prejudice in favour of old customs which is carried in everything to the greatest degree and must, as long as it continues, prove a great hindrance to all improvement.

The nearness of water to the surface accounts for the quick growth and great luxuriance of most of the trees in this country which in a short time afford good shade from the inclemency of the sun. There is one in particular wisely adopted for that purpose, the banyan tree. It has this peculiarity: it throws out roots from its principal branches (of the same appearance and fibred in the same way as ordinary roots are) which in time reach the ground and form a new trunk to support those shoots which the mother tree could not. I have seen one of these trees with one and twenty large trunks and a spread of branches that upwards of a thousand men might find shelter under. From its lofty, shady head, the banyan has a most majestic appearance that justly entitles it to be called the prince of the woods. It is an evergreen and bears a small red berry like our Flanders cherry, which is only food for birds. As it is useful, so is it plentiful, its natural beauty not requiring the addition of scarcity to make it esteemed. But though no tree can compare with this for beauty, yet for use the cocoa bears the palm. And deservedly does it claim the preference, as I believe there is none that ever supplied so many wants. It gives two kinds of liquor, one which is extracted by cutting off the heads of the bearing shoots, which distils a palatable kind of sharp, sweet liquor called toddy; the other is in the fruit, twice as large as a man's fist, which contains better than half a pint of a pleasing water. Both have the qualities of cooling and quenching thirst and are esteemed by the natives as very wholesome. There is a kind of kernel which sticks to the inward side of the shell and is, in taste, like our hazel nut, and an outward rind about an inch thick of a stringy substance which they spin into thread and use for sails and ropes. The shell makes good drinking vessels; the wood of the tree, though of a spongy nature, is made much use of in the construction of houses; and the leaves are used for covering. Thus every part of the tree is of service. Its form is not equal to its utility, consisting of a long bare trunk about thirty feet high, throwing out its fruit and leaves only at the head. When clustered, however, they afford good shade. The growth is not so quick as most others, as it takes about twelve years to come to maturity. But then it gives ample reward, for each tree brings its owner, when rented out, the value of eight shillings yearly.

I cannot pass on without mentioning another beautiful tree that abounds here, called by Europeans—because of its straightness and height—the mast tree. It much resembles our elm, with this difference, that it spreads its branches more regularly, ascends in a finer pyramid, and bears a fruit in appearance exactly like our damascene; but again only food for birds.

It would be endless to enumerate the variety of trees and plants to be found here, both for use and ornament. There are fruits of different kinds in abundance but they are not equal in flavour to the generality of those in Europe which I impute to the little pains that are taken to improve their culture as well as to the great quantity and long continuance of water about the roots in the wet season. This pushes on the growth too fast to permit them to arrive at that degree of perfection which a little pain would accomplish. The best and most wholesome fruit on this coast, according to my taste, is the plantain [a variety of banana], known in Europe by the name of the Indian fig. Every tree is the shoot of a year and they rise upwards of fourteen feet high with a stem of thirteen inches in circumference. After the fruit arrives at its maturity the shoot decays and a new one grows out of the old root. There is another species of the same fruit, called banana, but it is not equal to the first either in taste or flavour.

The mango is a tree that abounds here, generally very large and shady, bearing an abundance of fruit of the plum kind. But few in this latitude arrive at any degree of perfection. Those that do are extremely good and wholesome. There are likewise pineapples, oranges, lemons, limes, citrons, pomegranates, tamarinds and many more, not known in Europe even by name, most of them adapted to cool and to quench thirst. In short, such are the gifts of nature in this particular that anyone fond of gardening would find here ample subject to satisfy his curiosity, pleasure and profit. Many things, under the inspection of a curious hand, might be brought to their greatest degree of perfection—not even excepting European productions—in that way.

One might naturally conclude from the foregoing description of this part of the world that, where nature has so well done her part, its inhabitants ought to be happy. But so much do we have it in our power to spoil even her best gifts that here nineteen in twenty of the people are wretchedly miserable from the abominable government that prevails over this kingdom, which is nothing but a perfect scene of tyranny exerted from the highest in power to the lowest. I have heard a gentleman relate a circumstance which strongly exemplifies the foregoing observations. Being on his travels in the country, he saw a man beating another most severely. The second man made no resistance, which raised the gentleman's curiosity to enquire the cause, and he was informed that it was a rent-gatherer chastising a poor labourer because he had not wherewithal to pay his tax. This moved the gentleman's compassion, who gave him the money and so saved him from more stripes. With seeming ingratitude, the labourer went off without returning thanks and the gentleman pursued his journey. But, when out of sight of his persecutor, the poor fellow came to him and, with many thanks for his goodness, took out of his turban the equivalent of the sum lent in order to repay his benefactor. The gentleman refused it but desired to be told why the man, who had the money, would not sooner pay it than suffer the beating. The poor labourer answered that had he, at first asking, handed over the money, the rent-gatherer would have imagined that he had more besides and would therefore not have been satisfied with his due but would have searched and taken all the poor man's little hoard. Thus the inferior class are kept in extreme poverty, being constantly plundered by the stronger class who are, in their turn, plundered by their superiors, and so on to the very highest in power, who accumulates riches by the distress of his subjects.

Scarce can it be otherwise in a kingdom of so vast extent as this, where the viceroys are frequently too powerful and too far from the fountain-head to be chastised for any injustice or cruelty they may commit. Being sensible of this, they act with the less caution. The immediate delegates from the Mughal emperor are called nizams [actually, *subedars* or governors], of whom there are not above four or five in the whole kingdom. Their divisions are again subdivided and governed by nabobs who mostly hold their commissions from the nizams to whose province they belong. There are also rajas, or princes, who, being the ancient sovereigns of the country, are allowed by the Mughal to hold their principalities, paying a yearly tribute. But frequently they refuse and many are at this time independent, as are some of the nabobs.

The Moors who now govern this country are Muhammadans. The original inhabitants are pagans who are divided into a great number of castes or tribes, distinguished one from the other by a painted mark on the forehead. Each of these, according to their precedence, holds the others in great contempt, so much so that a person of superior caste thinks himself defiled if he even touches one of an inferior. The chief of all the tribes is the Brahmin caste, out of which alone come the priests. These, from the ignorance that prevails here, are held in great degree of veneration, though in general I take them to be a set of rogues whose principal view in their religion is self-interest. Yet there are numberless tales of incredible austerities suffered on account of religion. Perhaps some may be sincere, but from what I have hitherto heard and seen I may venture to say that few belong to that category.

There is a group of women set apart for the use of their religion. These are called dancing girls. They are debarred marriage, chosen for their beauty, employed to dance and sing before their pagodas, and otherwise serve the priests who—out of a charitable disposition—take care that they shall not die maids. In short, they are kind lasses, who more frequently cause the death of Europeans than the climate does. Though this is well known, one can resist their charms only with difficulty. The word 'charms' will probably surprise when applied to a black woman, but those who have seen their regular features, delicate shapes, wicked eyes, and dress wonderfully contrived to hide and yet show the body to the greatest advantage must allow the expression to be just. Their dress consists of a pair of long drawers that come as low as mid-leg; over that is a fine white muslin petticoat bound round the waist with a plate of silver; the shoulders and breasts are covered with a bodice of single satin, commonly crimson, that hides the colour but not the form of any thing and leaves bare about three inches of the small of the back; a thin veil of white gauze is thrown loose over this, of which, in their dances, they make a pretty use; their hair, which is always black and generally very long, is tied behind and hangs in a twisted tail ornamented with gold and jewels. But there is one part of their dress which custom has not reconciled me to, and I think never will, which is a large ring, generally a ruby, which hangs at one of their nostrils down to the upper lip. It disfigures them much and is scarcely made amends for by the good taste that is shown in the rest of their dress. They likewise wear necklaces, bracelets, shekels, and rings in their ears, on their fingers and toes, which deal of trinkets they make jingle to the time of their dance. This dress is particular to dancing girls. The rest of the sex have but a long piece of linen, uncut, part of which is rolled twice or thrice around the waist in the form of a petticoat, and the rest thrown over the breast and shoulders.

The clothing of the men consists in a white linen garment that lies close about the body and arms as low as the waist; from the waist it hangs in the form of a petticoat and touches the ground. It is bound round the middle with a sash, in which men of rank wear a dagger, called by them cress [kris]. The headdress is a turban. The pagans, but not the Moors, have rings in their ears and, some of them, in their nose. In general they let their beards grow, others grow whiskers only. Their dress, as that of the dancing girls, is a very becoming garb. The lower class of males go naked except for a little piece of linen in lieu of a fig leaf, and such is the force of custom that our European ladies here can look on a man in simple nature's dress with as little seeming emotion as they would on their grand dames in red mantles!

Both men and women chew betel. It is the leaf of a tree so named, in which is rolled a piece of a nut called arracka [areca], which looks like a nutmeg, a small quantity of fine lime, and an earth [wood extract] called Cutch [catechu] or Terra Japonica. The mixture is not unpleasant and I suppose, from the universal use that is made of it, custom has proved it to be wholesome. It colours the mouth and lips red. The natives are passionately fond of it and constantly use it.

To judge of the natives by their appearance, one naturally would be prejudiced in their favour. Their make is slight and genteel, their faces handsome, with such a look of mildness and innocence as induces one to conclude them an honest, inoffensive, harmless set of men. And such I am told is the real character of those who have not become conversant with Europeans. But in or near our settlements they have proved good scholars in vice, cheating and imposing without any restraint and, like their masters, sticking at nothing to enrich themselves. Their genius is sprightly and quick at learning and they have at the same time a sedateness of temper which makes even their children stick with indefatigable application to whatever they undertake. Many have made great proficiency in reading, speaking and writing English and in keeping accounts. They are employed by our factors in doing their business. The honesty of the uncorrupted natives cannot be better proved than in the confidence reposed in them both by white and black merchants, the common method of transmitting money from one end of the country to the other being by the seemingly poorest kind of peasant. The merchants will entrust them with as much as one or two thousand pounds and are, from long experience, in no way apprehensive of dishonesty or of their being in any way molested, for the fashionable vice of highway robbery has not as yet been transplanted to this part of the world.

The principal manufactures of this coast are muslin, calico and chintz in greatly varying degrees of fineness. Muslins are plain or of gold and silver, the latter being extremely handsome but very dear. Calicoes are prodigiously fine and of a dazzling whiteness. When painted, calico is called chintz and is valuable for the beauty of the colours, that brighten up by washing. These several manufactures, as most other things, have suffered prodigiously by the long continuance of the war, not being now in so high a degree of perfection nor anything like so cheap.

There are, here, most of the animals we have in Europe, and besides those, elephants, camels, buffaloes, tigers and jackals, the latter in great abundance, but no lions. The elephant bears a very great price, generally the value of about three hundred pounds sterling each, and costs for its daily sustenance upwards of eight shillings, so that none but men of the first rank and fortune can afford to keep them. Nor are they useful for lesser men, being mostly for parade and show, seldom carrying above three persons, two in a kind of wooden tower that is fixed on their back, and one that rides on the neck and—with a stick at the end of which is fixed a piece of iron resembling a coat hook—keeps them under surprising subjection. Those that are well broke in always kneel down for the keeper to get on their neck, or make a kind of step of one of their forefeet to help him up by. They pace or walk just as their governor directs and either way go very fast. I have seen one of fifteen feet high, but in general they do not exceed twelve.

The camels are used to carry burdens and are most useful in those hot regions, their particular quality being to go through great fatigue with little water and food. Their burden is commonly about six hundredweight, which they always kneel down to receive. If greater than what they can easily master is put on their back, they will not rise, but with their proper load they go over a great tract of ground.

In general the bullock and buffalo are what are made use of for carriage. These are in great plenty, it being one of the principal tenets of their religion not to kill either cow, bull, or buffalo which are held in a great degree of veneration. The woods abound with the wild boar, which is reckoned (and in my opinion very justly) the most delicate and wholesome food in the country. It resembles in taste our veal, but eats somewhat shorter [is more crumbly in texture] and yields a most rich gravy. The creature called jackal seems to me to be a wild dog, resembling it in everything and especially in the dismal yell so particular to that animal. They abound here and are excellent scavengers, picking up all that filth that might be

F

of dangerous consequence were it left to remain long exposed in a scorching sun. Night is the time they go in quest of prey, at which season they sally out in packs, setting up all together a most horrid yell that is answered from pack to pack all over the country, at first (with reason) terrifying any stranger who, however, soon grows accustomed to it after constant nightly repetition of the music.

Here abounds a variety of serpents and insects. One of the most venomous of the former, for whose bite no antidote has yet been found, is called the Covery capel [*cobra de capello*]. When angered it expands a kind of hood about its head that is handsomely varied with colours. There are several other serpents, all with most acute poisons. Amongst the variety of insects which swarm here, the luminous fly is not the least remarkable. It is of the beetle kind, near as large as a cricket, and shines by night very brightly, appearing, when flying, like so many stars—which produces a pretty effect. Birds there are many, but in general not of that fine plumage which I expected, and as for songsters there are few that deserve that name.

Animals which supply the table, both wild and tame, are in sufficient plenty: partridge, hares, quails, wild duck, teal, and snipe. The latter are as good as in Europe, but the others make in general dry food. The tame fowl are remarkably fine, in particular capons, which it is common to have as large as a middling turkey. Oxen and sheep are in general very small, very lean, and very bad, except for those they take the trouble to stall-feed, in which case they become excellent food but costly. Fish is moderately plentiful all along this coast, of various kinds, and many of them delicate eating, but Europeans do not esteem them as wholesome. Prawns are caught here from four to ten inches in length and good tasting. There are likewise oysters, in general very small and not worth the trouble of opening. Bread is tolerably good but very dear and often very scarce. No wheat growing on that coast, they are supplied with all they use from Bengal and Europe. The liquor is indifferent—arrack being our general drink—and not so good as in Europe owing to its being made use of too new and because it has not had the beneficial influence of a sea voyage. We have Madeira for about fifteen pence a quart, and a wine from Pondicherry which is called claret (though I believe that to be the smallest ingredient in it) for about half a crown. There is good claret sometimes to be had, commonly brought out by our English East India captains, at about five shillings a bottle.

On the whole, table expenses are costly in this country to Europeans, but very cheap to the natives, for their manner of living differs entirely from ours. Rice is their principal food and water their drink. With the rice they mix salt fish, greens and spice, but never touch spirituous liquor—a regimen that is undoubtedly properly adapted to the climate. Experience so far has evinced, past all doubt, that most of the deaths of our people are owing to their debauched lives, drunkenness and its attendant vices having been for the first months after their arrival a common practice notwithstanding the severest punishment used to deter them from it. Judge of the truth of the above assertion by the following return:

We landed on the coast, officers and privates, including the artillery	848
Dead in August 1755 of officers of our regiment and the artillery	8
D° . . . D° of privates of D° . . . D°	79
Total dead	87

Of which

Officers purely by the climate	1
D° of sickness begun by women	7
Privates by drunkenness and women	60
D° by the climate	11
D° by accidents	8
	87

From the above account I think we had no great reason to say that the climate is unhealthy. For, considering the trial a constitution must suffer in coming from 51° of latitude to 11, and the little care that was generally taken in seasoning our bodies to so great a change, I cannot say our loss was considerable, and I make no doubt, had we been sent on service in Europe, it would have been much more. Here are neither epidemical nor malignant disorders. The only one we suffered from was of the inflammatory sort which falls on the liver. Almost every one of our people that died had theirs corrupted. Excesses or venereal disorders commonly give rise to it and one is either dead or on the way to recovery in a week's time. [Medically induced] salivation is the common remedy but we have found it a desperate one, for if the treatment fails to produce spitting, it generally kills, sometimes quickly, sometimes by a slow decay. The case, I believe, is that those medicines which would be proper for this climate are not sufficiently looked for by our doctors. Probably what would be of service in Europe may have quite a different effect here, our bodies being relaxed and not able to undergo any serious operation.

I have now, my dear Father, laid before you a short, connected account of this expedition until July 1756, with a description of the places I saw and the observations I made on the country, climate and customs of these people, although my ignorance of their language has prevented it from being so full and satisfactory as I should wish and must always be a principal impediment to relations of this kind. As the scene of action is shortly to change, I shall make that the subject of a second part.

PART
TWO

CHAPTER FIVE

In July 1756, though everything was in a state of tranquillity on the coast of Coromandel between the English and the French, yet the probability of a rupture induced the Company to carry on the new fortifications at Madras with great vigour and despatch. The garrison then was for that part of the world numerous and good, made up of the best part of the Company's troops and all our regiment, exclusive of those on board the fleet which then lay in the road before the town—the *Kent* of sixty guns, the *Cumberland* of seventy, the *Tyger* of sixty, the *Salisbury* fifty, the *Bridgewater* twenty, and a small fireship. Thus circumstanced, the Company were able not only to defend themselves from any attempt by the French but might have acted offensively against an enemy [the Marathas] that has for some years past been considerably increasing its power to our detriment. This probably would have been the case had not the unexpected news from Bengal opened a new scene of action and determined their fluctuating resolutions.

The great and rich province of Bengal is situated at the

bottom of a bay of the same name. It is governed by a nabob who, according to the institution established by the Moors, is but a vicegerent of the Mughal and ought to be appointed by him. But these nabobs, through their riches, power, and distance from their king, generally shake off the yoke and become independent. In the country of Bengal the English, French, Dutch and Danes have factories [trading centres] that are of great consequence to each nation, not only as being the principal mart for most kinds of merchandise but because from there they supply their other settlements (chiefly on the coast of Coromandel) with rice and wheat. The most considerable, belonging to the English, is called Calcutta, besides which they have other subordinate ones at Cassenbuzar [Kasimbazar] near Muxidavad [Murshidabad], the metropolis of the province, Patna, Decka [Dacca], and some few other places. They were much superior in point of trade and riches to any other of the European nations and enjoyed many privileges above them while the country was ruled by Alivardi Khan, a nabob of great military capacity and a great politician, whose qualities had early induced him to shake off his dependence on the Mughal. He became free and uncontrolled master of that extensive province. I cannot pretend to assign the first cause of the ensuing troubles, not having proper materials to direct me to truth through the many different, contradictory accounts that prevail concerning it. I shall therefore confine myself to that which latterly, as is most generally allowed, determined the nabob to act as he did.

Alivardi Khan had appointed one Raja Bullub [Rai Durlabh] as his agent at Dacca. This man, through some malversation in his government or court intrigue, had been summoned to appear at Murshidabad, in order to give an account of his administration. Either through a consciousness of having done something he could not answer for, or fearful that right or wrong he would be stripped of his wealth, he sent it with his son, called Kissendas [Krishna Das] to Calcutta in hopes that both would be safe under the protection of the English who had previously given their promise to receive him. At this time, the old Nabob Alivardi Khan died and was succeeded in his government on 9 April 1756 by his grandson [grandnephew], Surajud Doulat [Siraj-ud-daula], whom he had adopted as his successor. No sooner had the new nabob taken the reins of government in his hands than he sent an ambassador to Mr Drake, governor of Calcutta, and the Council, requiring Krishna Das and the treasure to be delivered up. They readily would have resigned the man but, claiming not to know anything of the treasure (a point which seems to admit of many doubts) and imagining the nabob would make a handle of it to exact money from them, they not only refused his demand but, with unparalleled insolence, flogged his ambassador and ignominiously turned him out of the town. This undoubted provocation, joined to many other reasons of complaint, roused the young nabob to a determination of humbling the insolence of the English and, being then at the head of a numerous army intended to do battle with his old enemy the Nabob of Purneah, he altered his destination and laid siege to their small fort of Kasimbazar at the beginning of June.

This news arrived at Madras in August and two hundred men under the command of Major Kilpatrick were immediately sent to assist. But, by the intelligence that arrived shortly after their departure, it appeared that the nabob's despatch was such as to render the reinforcement of no effect. For he took possession of Kasimbazar on 5 June 1756 and was at Calcutta on the 16th. In this interval he had marched upwards of one hundred miles and crossed the Ganges several times with an army of

100,000 men as well as a considerable train of artillery. Such was his despatch and such the neglect of the English that he was in front of their town before they even knew he had begun his march.

From such a beginning there was no great room to flatter onesself with a vigorous defence and indeed, even had those in Calcutta been so disposed, the badness of their fortification, their want of all kind of ammunition and stores, and the small number of their troops (consisting of about fifty military), as well as their being entirely destitute of a proper head to conduct them in such circumstances, rendered it almost impossible. The appearance of the nabob's army threw them into the utmost confusion and, instead of collecting their small force within their fort and resting satisfied with defending that, they ineffectually attempted securing part of the town in a circuit of near two miles. This, after having considerably lessened their number, they were obliged to abandon and at last took refuge within walls that wanted everything to make them defensible. Here they were again closely pursued and vigorously attacked, for it is the nature of these black troops that the least advantage gained makes them press on with prodigious ardour. Retired now to their last refuge, the English—instead of dividing their people so that each might have an equal share of labour and rest—fell into a state of confusion and anarchy. The governor [Roger Drake] so far from exerting himself on this occasion in view of the desperate situation of affairs and the turn they seemed likely to take, shamefully abandoned his fort and took shelter on board one of the ships that then lay in the river. His example was soon followed by all who could get boats so that none stayed in the fort but those who were compelled to it by necessity. These few, being soon worn down with fatigue and not able to keep watch, gave an opportunity to the Moors to make themselves masters of the place by escalade. This took place on 20 June 1756, after a siege of four days.

The English who were taken prisoner were at first treated with more humanity than is generally shown on like occasions, for they had liberty to walk where they pleased in the town. But some of the [English] soldiers getting drunk the same evening, abusing and quarrelling with the Moors, complaints were made to the nabob who ordered all the Europeans into confinement. This was immediately put into execution by cramming the whole, consisting of about 230 men [in fact, 146], into a place that had served as a black-hole [confinement cell] for the punishment of soldiers. This prison being much too small for that number and having but one window to admit fresh air, in the morning there were but twenty-four [23] of the whole left alive.

This was looked upon as the greatest act of barbarism, but it was with injustice laid to the nabob's charge. His orders, in the then situation of affairs, were no more than what any general would have done. Certainly, the person to whom he entrusted the execution of them was not clear of blame, it being his duty to have examined the place before the prisoners were put in. But instead, he only enquired what was the usual place of confinement in the fort and was correctly shown the black-hole. So he thrust the whole of those poor people in to a scene of horror and distress not to be described. The calamity of the surviving wretches being made known to the nabob, he immediately ordered them to be released, except the chiefs, whom he still kept in confinement.

Those who had escaped out of the fort before it was taken had withdrawn down the river some sixty miles, on board a few ships that then lay there, to a place called Fulta. Here they were unmolested but obliged to keep on board where, from a want of almost all the necessaries of life, they were driven to the greatest distress, a situation doubly felt by people who shortly before had lived in all the affluence and pleasure that riches and a free gratification of most of their passions could procure. By leaving them in the river, it appears that the nabob's intentions were not entirely to banish the English from his dominions but only to bring them to a greater state of submission and dependence. He might effectually have rooted them out with much more ease and less risk than he had exposed himself to in taking their fort.

During these transactions, the rest of the European settlements had remained neutral spectators of the nabob's successes, either from dread of his power or from a secret desire to see humbled their superiors in trade and riches.

This was the situation of affairs at the arrival of Major Kilpatrick, but the forces he had brought were insufficient to attempt anything and he was obliged to remain inactive with the poor remains of the settlement collected at Fulta, a small Dutch settlement on the same river as Calcutta but sixty miles nearer the sea, until succour came from Madras, now the only source from which assistance could be expected.

The regaining of their possessions in Bengal was of too great consequence to all the other British settlements for them not to make the greatest efforts to effect it, but, as Madras was the nearest, it was best able to exert itself on the occasion. Greatly were they divided, and long did they spend in determining on the troops and commander that should be sent on this important expedition, which gave rise to many resolutions and as many alterations in the debates of their committee. The king's regiment and artillery under the command of Colonel Adlercron were at first fixed on, then they were changed for Company troops under the command of Lieutenant-Colonel Clive. Thus they fluctuated for several days, to the just mortification of our colonel, who either should never have been mentioned for the expedition or—once fixed on and his consent obtained, as was the case—the matter should not have been altered. At last it was determined that the whole fleet and two Indiamen, with about six hundred Europeans and two thousand sepoys (black soldiers in the Company's pay), under the command of Colonel Clive, should proceed with all despatch to attempt the recovery of the lost settlement. The detachment of our regiment that was then on board was there for the use of the ships and therefore could not be landed unless others were sent in their place. This none desired or asked, as it was the only service we had been called to since our arrival in India.

The first account of the loss of Calcutta was received at Madras some time in August 1756, but because of the forementioned irresolutions and delays it was the middle of October before everything was ready for the expedition. This was of the utmost consequence and near frustrated all attempted action, for in this bay there are regular monsoon winds that blow from the north-east from October to March, with strong currents setting according to the wind. The committee's dilatoriness brought us to a season in which we had to attempt a voyage against wind and current and to think ourselves happy to accomplish in two months what in the proper time of year is generally done in six days.

Everything at last accomplished and the troops embarked, we sailed from Madras on 16 October 1756. The sepoys, on account of some particular forms in their religion, were a long time before they could be persuaded to undertake such a voyage but by fair promises they were at last prevailed upon and most of them put on board the two India ships that accompanied us. Their priests, ever watchful over what may conduce to their advantage, received from each of these poor ignorant people a considerable sum of money to render their gods propitious and grant them a speedy and good passage.

CHAPTER SIX

We soon had reason to perceive that a voyage attempted against wind and current was not likely to be easily accomplished, for such was the speed we made that, on the 19th, we found ourselves in sight of the island of Ceylon—some degrees further south of our destined port than we had been when we set out. There we met with the usual weather off that land, squalls, rains and calms, which prevented our quitting sight of the island until the 21st, after which foul wind and bad weather were our constant attendants. On 13 November we were alarmed by guns of distress from the *Salisbury*, occasioned by her having sprung a leak in her wooden ends that filled two inches more than all her pumps could clear as we were sailing against a large head sea. We lay to, but the next day it was found on examination not to be of so dangerous a consequence as was at first imagined.

Until the 25th, everything seemed to go counter to our wishes, but then a fair wind and fine weather again revived our drooping spirits. Thus we continued until the 30th when, in latitude 20° 24′ about six in the evening, we

G

struck soundings with seventy-fathom line on what we imagined to be the sea reef, which is a bank of land lying to the eastwards of Balasore road and generally made by all ships on their entrance. With constant soundings and a bold sail we proceeded, the *Kent* leading, and the *Cumberland* (the ship I was in) according to station on her larboard quarter. At nine at night on 1 December we had fifteen-fathom water. About ten minutes later, the conner [look-out] said with an oath that we were aground! Immediately we sounded and found a quarter less four, just the water we drew.

Then all was uproar: down sails and anchor (a dangerous thing in our situation), hoist lights and fire guns, signals to prevent the following ships falling into the same danger. But before all this was accomplished, we very sensibly struck several times. The boats were immediately hoisted out to find the deepest water and in searching for it they perceived breakers about half a mile ahead. About one o'clock the tide seemed to leave us, for we felt the ground more sensibly and, the sky beginning to lower and danger pressing, we cut our cable, set sail, and steered near the same point we came in at. When under sail we rubbed the ground several times but at last got into deep water and, about two o'clock, cast anchor with our best bow-anchor in seven fathom and a half. The whole fleet, on our signal, did the same. The *Kent* had been about a league ahead, we steering by her lights, but the fact of our having steering sails set occasioned a difference in our course of two or three miles, by which means we ran upon danger which she escaped.

In the morning we perceived that we had been greatly out in our reckoning, for instead of being on the sea reef, as we imagined, we were in sight of Palmyras point (then bearing west by south), and could see breakers very little ahead of the place where we struck. This was on a bank that runs out some leagues from that point, low land with a few trees on it. Luckily, there being smooth water and little wind, we received no perceivable damage.

On the 2nd, the *Kent* set sail, steering for Balasore as she had already passed the bank. We and the rest of the fleet waited for the tide, and weighed about two in the afternoon. The *Tyger* and *Walpole*, one of the Indiamen, being somewhat more to windward than us, cleared the bank, but the *Cumberland*, the *Salisbury* and the twenty-gun ship [*Bridgewater*] could not accomplish it. On the 3rd we made a second attempt but with no better success than before. On the 4th, the wind and swell rising, we continued at anchor. On the 5th, the swell from the south-east and wind from the north-east Increased to such a degree as to cause our cable to part about four o'clock in the morning. We immediately got under sail and stood to the south-east. Shortly after, we saw the *Salisbury* and *Bridgewater* also under sail, but before ten they were out of sight. We had now lost two of our best anchors and only one of those remaining was stocked; our leak, which the ship had long complained of in her wooden ends, was so considerably enlarged by bearing against the swell that it kept two chain-pumps constantly at work; the number of sick had increased prodigiously, being now upwards of 150; our fresh stocks, the admiral's not excepted, were entirely gone; and we had rice and water for but twelve days at short allowance. Briefly, our situation bore a dismal aspect in every respect. The golden expectations some had flattered themselves with at the beginning of the expedition now began to vanish, supplanted by hungry bellies and what sailors call a smart gale.

The bad weather continued until 7 December, then cleared up, when observation showed us to be in 20° 14′ north. We persisted in attempting our passage and on the 8th struck soundings with fifty-fathom line on the bank off Palmyras point but, the current being strong against us, we anchored about two in the afternoon. On the 9th we weighed and saw the land which is called the 'false point' [twenty-four miles south of Palmyras point], by which we found we had lost ground by the last attempt. The next day, becalmed and with the current running against us, we still fell to leeward. With our sick now increased to 225, with water and provisions for not above seven days, and with the men who were not yet sick so weak as to be scarce able to work the ship, Admiral Pocock determined to bear away for Vizagapatam, which we accordingly did at twelve o'clock.

Thus did we experience in full, through two months' navigation, the bad consequences attending the delays at Madras. Wind and current being in our favour for our new destination, however, we arrived and anchored in the road of Vizagapatam on 14 December at six in the evening. We had about fifty men free from sickness out of 730, and but one butt of water. Judge therefore what we must have suffered and how just were our apprehensions.

Our first care here was in getting the sick ashore. Many of them died in the attempt, or shortly after (being then in the last stage of the scurvy), notwithstanding that everything was done that could contribute to their recovery.

Vizagapatam lies in north latitude 17° 43' and was hitherto the principal settlement the English had in the kingdom of Golconda. Here they kept a chief, a second, and a writer, and but a very poor garrison. However, it was fully sufficient for the defence of the fortifications they had, which could make no manner of resistance against a European power and but a poor one even against the forces of the country. Yet one would imagine it of consequence enough to deserve a little more attention as, from this place, they were supplied with most of their long cloth, the investments, the year we were there, amounting

to 1500 bales, each of which contained about eighty
pieces. With proper encouragement, a much greater
quantity could be furnished. This commodity is cheap
and very fine here, and their chintz is esteemed the best in
India for the brightness of its colours. The place is likewise remarkable for its inlay work, and justly, for they do
it to the greatest perfection.

On the whole there appeared to me greater signs of in-
dustry and ingenuity amongst these people than in any
other place fallen under my observation in India. The face
of this country likewise differs much from that of most
other parts on the coast of Coromandel, abounding with
mountains and delightful valleys. I shall attempt to
picture it out by an account of a little excursion made on
12 January 1757 to a remarkable place called the Sumatra
pagoda, about twelve miles inland. We set out at six in the
morning and by seven arrived at Annamanta vale, so
called from being the resort of monkeys [Hanuman: the
monkey god]—the signification of that word in their
language. It is situated between two high and steep hills
that are covered with trees except here and there where
there is a cragged rock showing its head through the different shades of green which the infinite variety of nature
has produced here. Through the middle of the vale lies a
clear and purling stream, affording superior delight in
warm climes, nourishing and increasing that luxuriance
of growth which abounds in these parts, and constantly
keeping a green and pleasing carpet with a number of
shady groves—charming shelter for a country party! The
prospect is closed in one direction by hills that rise in
amphitheatre to a great height, covered in the same
manner as those at the entrance. From the other extremity
you have a distant prospect of the sea, the whole together
making one of those pleasing, rural prospects which diffuse
an unspeakable calm delight on the mind of man.

Under one of these groves we breakfasted and then proceeded on our journey through a second vale, still beautiful, but much more extensive than the former. It is well inhabited and well improved. At about ten we arrived at the bottom of the mountain on whose brow the pagoda is built. There are the remains of a large gateway which, by its ruins, appears to have been very extensive. The way up is by stone stairs, in number above eight hundred and at present much out of repair. On ascending the mountain, a more extensive vale than either of the former opens to view, encircled by woody hills except for an opening at the extremity where the sight is lost in a similar country. Half way up is a second gateway and a small pagoda containing the figure of an enormous monkey cut in the rock. From then on up to Sumatra village and the pagoda is nothing remarkable. The pagoda at present has little worth observation. Its architecture is the same as that all over the country. The pillars, which are of a very fine, bluish stone, are carved with a multitude of different figures tolerably well executed. Almost every stone has some characters cut on it which, according to the best information we could get, are only records of the men of rank who have been there from devotion to give alms. As we could not get in to the inward part of the temple, I cannot say what figure they worship, but in the outer hall is a large one of a man kneeling on one knee and another of a monkey in the same attitude. There are heaps of ruins for some distance about the principal building by which it seems to have been much more considerable than it at present appears. As to its age we could get little satisfaction, only that it was of a very long standing, had been five generations abuilding, and that there had been four floods since it was completed.

A little distance from the pagoda is a *choultry* built over a fine and plentiful spring, probably the principal inducement to their fixing on that solitary situation. Here we spent the heat of the day and in the evening ascended the utmost summit of the mountain which, being one of the highest in the country, amply rewarded us for the fatigue of the walk. The extensive prospect it yielded on all sides entertained the sight with a country where nature seemed to have spread her gifts with a very liberal hand. Even the highest land here produces a kind of grain particularly adapted to dry situations, which throws out a stem of sixteen or seventeen feet bearing a large head full of small seed resembling millet, with which the peasants make bread.

We lay in the *choultry* that night and, on the 13th, descended the mountain and traversed part of the plain which showed to so much advantage from the rising ground. Here we found our sight had not deceived us, for throughout our whole walk to a small country fort called Norway we pursued our way through cornfields of plenteous crops, fine plantations of cotton and tobacco, pasture plains well stocked with cattle, and villages seemingly well inhabited. After satisfying our curiosity at Norway, where there is nothing worth notice, we finished our excursion that evening.

Shortly after our arrival at Vizagapatam, we had the first account of a French war [in Europe]. This much alarmed the chief of the settlement, for Mr Bussy and a considerable French army had long been masters of that part of the country and probably now would attempt to dispossess the English of all their factories there. Induced by these apprehensions, the chief requested Admiral Pocock to leave there most of the Company troops he had on board his ship. The admiral consented, not purposing then to proceed to Bengal, and accordingly landed upwards of one hundred—which you will find, by the sequel, answered no other end than to lose the use of that number of men for the rest of the war.

In the beginning of February 1757 we had some imperfect account from Bengal of our successes there, which I presume induced Admiral Pocock to imagine his presence would now be needless, it being likely that Admiral Watson would have left Bengal before we could arrive. Therefore, the sick being pretty well recovered, we weighed anchor on the 5th and sailed for Madras. The currents at this time of the year beginning to change, and the winds to be variable, it was the 21st before we reached our port.

Here we had confirmation of our successes and a more ample account of the situation of affairs in Bengal. The whole fleet, after enduring much hardship, had all arrived safe in Bengal except our own ship. At Fulta they found the poor remains of the settlement in the utmost distress, for besides the many difficulties they had to encounter a mortality had swept off the greatest number of them. Those belonging to the detachment that went with Major Kilpatrick felt the effects of it particularly severely. But soon the face of affairs was altered. On 24 December the fleet and the land forces under Colonel Clive attacked a fort of the nabob's called Budge Budge, which they took the same day, though it was very strong and, if well defended, would have been capable of giving them much trouble. They pursued their blow and, on 3 January 1757, attacked and re-took Calcutta. At both places they sustained but little loss. Not satisfied with this, the day after taking Calcutta, part of the troops—under the command of Major Kilpatrick, with the twenty-gun ship [*Bridgewater*], *Kingfisher* sloop, and some boats—proceeded higher up the river to a rich Moorish town called Hugli. In their progress thither, the *Bridgewater* ran on a bank and was three days before she could be got off, which gave time to the inhabitants to remove their most valuable effects. After a siege of twenty-four hours they took the fort,

demolished it, and plundered the town in a most unmerciful manner in retaliation for what had passed at
Calcutta. The rapidity of these successes astonished the
nabob who, with a numerous army, marched down to the
English settlement with the same despatch he had done at
first and arrived there the 1st February. His approach
altered the face of affairs with our people for, from having
plenty of all things, they now were reduced to the utmost
distress, the nabob having forbidden any kind of provisions to be brought into our camp. This made it necessary for some bold stroke to be undertaken either to dis-
lodge him or to oblige him to come to terms.

The nabob's forces were encamped round the town in a
place that had a good rampart and a ditch on the country
side. The latter had been made by the English some years
before as a defence against the incursions of the Marathas.
Our army—in number about 1200 Europeans including
sailors and 2000 [in fact, 800] sepoys—were encamped
about three miles from them. Thus were they situated
when Colonel Clive formed the resolution of attacking the
nabob's camp, a bold and daring undertaking but a
necessary one. The plan was put in execution on 5
February 1757. After leaving a very small detachment to
defend their own camp, they marched out at two o'clock
in the morning and arrived at the skirts of the nabob's
before daybreak. They entered it with great success, but a
most prodigious thick fog arising so much baffled the
skill of their guide as to make them mistake the road to the
nabob's quarters. This was their principal aim and, had
they reached it, they would probably have put an end to
the war. Instead of that, they marched in front of the
rampart behind which his army and cannon were lodged.
This mistake gave the Moors time to recover from the
panic which at first seized them, and they began to annoy
our people most terribly with a heavy fire of cannon and

small arms. What made it still more dismal was that our men could make no return, the enemy being quite under cover. In these circumstances, a considerable body of enemy horse made an attack, but by the thickness of the fog did not see our men until they almost touched their bayonets and received so close and heavy a fire as brought most of them down and obliged the few remaining to retreat.

The colonel, now perceiving his scheme had miscarried, resolved to make a path through the ditch and rampart in order to get into the town, from which he could communicate with his camp. This seemed less hazardous than to return the way he came. Accordingly it was done, though its execution was much galled by the enemy who pursued him all the way. He arrived about eleven in the morning, having had killed and wounded in the whole affair more than two hundred men [in fact, 194]. This, by appearance, seemed rather a defeat than a victory but in its consequences proved the latter, for the nabob was frightened by the boldness of the attack and the danger he had escaped. The number of his people slain and wounded, by their own account, amounted to upward of 1500, and he retired from his camp the night after and agreed to a suspension of arms which terminated in the following treaty.

ARTICLES acceded to and signed by the Nabob of Bengal, 9th February 1757.

1st Whatever rights and privileges the King [Mughal emperor] has granted the English Company in their Phirmaund [*firman*, charter] and the Hulhoorums [*hosbolhookum*, document of royal authorisation] sent from Delly [Delhi], shall not be disputed or taken from them, and the immunities therein mentioned be acknowledged and stand good: Whatever villages are

given to the Company by the Phirmaund shall likewise be granted notwithstanding they have been
denied by former Subahs [*subedar*, Mughal provincial governor], the Zemindars [landholders] of
those villages not to be hurt or displaced without
cause.

    Signed by the Nabob in his own hand:
        'I agree to the terms of the Phirmaund'

2d All goods passing and repassing through the country
by land or water with the English dustucks [permits]
shall be exempt from any tax, fee or imposition, from
Chokeys [customs officers], Gaulwall [warehouse
keepers], Zemindars or any others.
        'I agree to this'

3d All the Company's factories seized by the Nabob shall
be returned. All monies, goods and effects belonging
to the Company, their servants and Tenants, and
which have been seized and taken by the Nabob, shall
be restored. What has been plundered and pillaged by
his people made good by the payment of such a sum
of money as his justice shall think reasonable.
        'I agree to restore whatever has been seized and
        taken by my orders and accounted for in my
        sircary [ledgers]'

4th That we have permission to fortify Calcutta in such
manner as we may think proper without interruption.
        'I consent to this'

5th That we shall have liberty to coin siccas [new coins]
both gold and silver, of equal weight and fineness of
those of Muxidavad [Murshidabad] which shall pass
in the provinces.
        'I consent to the English Company's coining
        their own imports of bullion and gold into
        Siccas'

6th That a Treaty shall be ratified by signing and sealing,

and swearing to abide by the articles therein contained, not only by the Nabob, but by his principal officers and Ministers.

> 'I have sealed and signed the articles before the presence of God'

7th That Admiral Charles Watson and Colonel Robert Clive on the part and behalf of the English nation and of the Company do agree to live in a good understanding with the Nabob, to put an end to these troubles, and be in friendship with him while these articles are performed and observed by the Nabob.

> 'I have sealed and signed the foregoing articles upon these terms: That if the Governour and Council will Sign and Seal them with the Company's seal, and will swear to the performance on their part, I then consent and agree to them'.

Which was accordingly done.

CHAPTER SEVEN

Thus were the English after an eight months' banishment restored again to their settlement, and not only to the full enjoyment of their ancient rights and privileges but many more. As the fleet had principally contributed thereto, so was it necessary it should stay some time longer to see the ratification of the treaty. Furthermore, the French war was now known in those parts and there was a scheme on foot towards dispossessing them of their settlements.

Being informed of these matters, Admiral Pocock resolved to join the fleet as soon as possible and we left Madras on 1 March 1757. Here we had a remarkable instance of the good effect of attending proper seasons to make voyages in these seas, for now, having the monsoon for us, we accomplished in five days, with all our men in perfect health, that which we could not previously do, with sickness and distress, in nine weeks.

On our arrival at the entrance of the river Ganges, which is above one hundred miles from Calcutta, the place where the fleet lay, we were informed that an expedition against Chandernagore (the chief settlement belonging to the French, on the same river about thirty miles higher up) was determined on and immediately to be put into execution. We likewise heard that a few days before we had received a reinforcement from Bombay of upwards of two hundred men [in fact, 400]. The same messenger brought orders for the troops on board the *Cumberland* to repair with all speed to Calcutta. But as our men were absolutely necessary for the working of the ship in the intricate navigation at the entrance to and up this river, we were detained on board some days for that purpose. Admiral Pocock and Captain Grant, who was the commanding officer of our detachment, went on in the meantime, but it was the 23rd before the rest could be despatched—consisting of one lieutenant, one ensign, three serjeants, two drummers, and eighty-six rank and file, all in health and fit for duty, no small reinforcement.

We arrived at Calcutta the 24th, where we were informed that Chandernagore had surrendered the previous day after an obstinate defence. The land army had begun the attack on the 14th, but the ships had not come before the settlement until the day it was taken. The *Kent*, in which were Admiral Watson and Captain Speke, and the *Tyger* with Admiral Pocock and Captain Latham, were by some mistake or neglect the only ships that suffered, or indeed the only ones within shot. Each of them had upwards of twenty men killed and seventy wounded [in fact, thirteen and fifty on the *Tyger*, and nineteen and forty-nine on the *Kent*]. The *Kent* had likewise two lieutenants killed and was so much hurt in her hull, masts and rigging, that she had shortly after to be laid up. On board each ship was the allotted detachment of our regiment which had been landed during all the earlier service done ashore but was again embarked on this occasion. By

the testimony of everyone, they behaved with remarkable
spirit and resolution.

The French had in the fort, besides sepoys, near five
hundred Europeans collected from all their ships, many
being at that time in the river. Two they sunk in the
channel in hopes of preventing our men-of-war coming
up. Three or four would effectually have done so. Here I
cannot help observing the boldness of this undertaking
which, to cool, unprejudiced reason, seemed to abound
with almost insurmountable difficulties. The river, rapid
and navigationally dangerous, was not known to any of
our pilots higher up than Calcutta, and in many places
formed a very narrow channel. There were some strong
batteries on the water's edge, and a boom across the river.
As well as all this, the fort to be attacked was pretty strong,
well supplied with everything, and well garrisoned. But
the principal springs of this undertaking were spirits not
to be daunted by any difficulties, and experience proved
their strength equal to their resolution.

The policy of the French in the transaction of earlier
affairs seems somewhat extraordinary. Had they sided
with the nabob at the time he came down to oppose the
successes of the English—as they might have done, being
then informed of the war—it is probable we should never
have attacked their settlement and perhaps not even have
been able to re-establish ourselves. But instead of pursuing
what was apparently so much their interest, they remained
neutral spectators of our rapid conquests, buoying themselves up with the notion that neutrality would subsist in
the river in this war, as had ever been the case before—for
none of the former nabobs would allow of any act of
hostility between the English and French in their dominions. Indeed, Siraj-ud-daula wrote to the former peremp-
torily not to attempt anything against the latter—nay,
sent an army to see his orders fulfilled. But they, hearing

on their march of the reduction of the place, turned back. So little did we, even at that time, mind his menaces, and such was the opinion our successes had already given of our arms.

The booty taken in the fort was pretty considerable, amounting to upwards of eight lakhs [*lakh*, 100,000] of rupees, or £96,000, with great quantity of all kinds of warlike stores. Furthermore, about ten French ships were destroyed and between three and four hundred prisoners taken, many others having escaped at the time the flag of truce was hung out.

The following are the articles of capitulation signed on that occasion.

ARTICLES of Capitulation for Fort D'Orleans of Chandernagore proposed by Peter Renault Esqr Director General, and the Gentlemen of the Council for the French East India Company's affairs, to Charles Watson Esqr Vice Admiral of the Blue Squadron of his Britannic Majesty's Fleet, and Commander in Chief of all his Majesty's Ships and Vessels employed in the East Indies, and of the marine Forces of the United Company of Merchants trading to and in these parts; with the Admiral's answer thereto. March the 23rd 1757—

1st The lives of all deserters shall be saved.

ANSW: The deserters to be absolutely given up

2d All the Officers of this Garrison shall be prisoners on their parole of honour; that they shall have liberty to carry with them all their effects, and go where they please, on promising they will not serve against his Britannic Majesty during the present war.

ANSW: The Admiral agrees to.

3d The Soldiers of the garrison shall be prisoners of war, so long as the present war continues; and when a peace is made between the King of France and the

King of England, they shall be sent to Pondicherry,
and till then be entertained at the expense of the
English Company.

> ANSW: The Admiral likewise agrees.—with this
> difference only, that, instead of sending the
> Soldiers to Pondicherry, they shall be sent
> to Madras, or to England, as the Admiral
> shall hereafter think proper; and that such
> foreigners, who are not of the French nation
> and choose voluntarily to enter into the
> English Service shall have liberty

4th The Seapoys of the garrison shall not be prisoners of
war; they shall have leave on the contrary, to return
on the coast in their Country.

> ANSW: The Admiral agrees to

5th The Officers and men of the Company's European
Ship *St Contest* shall be sent to Pondicherry in the
first English Ship which goes to the coast.

> ANSW: The Officers and Men of the European Ship
> shall be upon the same footing as the
> Soldiers, and to be sent to Madrass or to
> England as soon as possible.

6th The French Jesuit fathers shall have liberty to exercise
the function of their religion in the house which has
been assigned them since the demolishing of their
church: the Silver ornaments, and everything that
belongs to the Church shall be given them, and also
their effects.

> ANSW: The Admiral cannot agree to any Euro-
> peans residing here, but, that the French
> Jesuits may go to Pondicherry with all the
> ornaments of their Church or wherever
> they please.

7th All the Inhabitants of what nation or quality soever,
as Europeans, Mustees [half-castes], Christians, Blacks,

H

Gentils, Moors, and others, shall be put in possession of their houses, and all in general as shall be found belonging to them, either in the Fort, or on their estates.

ANSW: In regard to this Article, to be left to the Admiral, who will do justice.

8th The Factories at Cassembuzar, Decca, Patna, Jenda, and Ballasore, shall remain at the command of the Chiefs who direct them.

ANSW: To be settled between the Nabob and the Admiral.

9th The Directors, Counsellors, and those employed under them, shall have leave to go where they please, with their cloaths and linen.

ANSW: The Admiral agrees to.

The Admiral expects an answer by three o'clock this afternoon, and, that the British forces may take possession of the Fort by four.

The above mentioned propositions have been accepted of by the Council in consequence of which we have delivered up the fortress of Chandernagore to Admiral Watson.

Chandernagore the 23rd March 1757

P. Renault

Laportiere   M. Fournier

F. Nicola   A. Caillott

Sugues

Colonel Clive not being mentioned in the foregoing articles created a coolness between him and the admiral ever after.

After the reduction of the place, the army encamped about two miles from the town. I joined them with the detachment on 26 March 1757, and was the next day appointed by Colonel Clive to act as captain.

We remained in this camp about five weeks but, as it appeared to give umbrage to the nabob that we should keep the field when everything was settled in the country, we were ordered into quarters to free his mind from all suspicion. Accordingly we marched into Chandernagore on 3 May 1757, the town and fort being allotted as quarters.

The English now recovered that character which their pusillanimous behaviour at Calcutta had justly lost them, and were once more looked on as a great and powerful people. At present this was nothing more than their due, for their forces here were considerable—a strong fleet, a tolerably disciplined army of near eight hundred Europeans, three hundred [in fact, 100] topasses [Eurasian soldiers], three thousand sepoys [2100] and a good train of artillery. Nor was there any European power to compete. Thus situated, with minds still angered against the nabob, the tempting opportunity of pursuing further revenge could not be withstood. Therefore they tampered with one of the leading men of his court, Jafir Ally Cawn [Mir Jafar], a distant relation to the family on the throne, offering him the nabobship provided he would lend assistance to dethrone his master. The man was of a good character and generally liked, but the bait was too powerful for Eastern honesty to withstand and, though he would not yet openly join us, he promised to do it as soon as an opportunity offered. In case of success and the fulfilling of our promise, he promised to give a million sterling to the Company, half a million to the navy and army, and half a million to make good the private sufferings of Calcutta, with a further donation as particular reward to the chiefs in this undertaking.

Thus intentioned and on these premises we prepared everything for a march to Murshidabad, the nabob's capital. Our army was as above mentioned, with six pieces of cannon—all short sixes—one hobit [howitzer], and fifty seamen whom the admiral spared us. The cause of this undertaking was given out to be on account of the nabob's not having fulfilled many articles of the late treaty.

This expedition to many seemed desperate, as it must to everyone who has not a thorough knowledge of these people. With an army which in Europe would be called but a handful of men, we attempted to dethrone a monarch who ruled a greater extent of country than most European kings, and as well peopled; whose revenue amounted to three millions; and who could at all times assemble upwards of one hundred thousand fighting men, with cannon in proportion. The march proposed was above one hundred miles, through a country full of rivers and at a season of the year when the rains that flood almost the whole land are expected to fall. These difficulties at first view must seem almost insurmountable and justly make us regarded as madmen to have attempted it. But when we come to consider, on the other hand, the great want of discipline in this country; the tyrannical government that prevails, which makes one tyrant as good as another and each man's property neither more nor less secure as a result of change; the lack of constitution making liberty everyone's concern; and, according to accounts, a most general dissatisfaction on the part of the great with the then nabob; when all this is considered it does not seem quite so rash an undertaking.

Another inducement in vindication of this step, however desperate it might appear, was that the French, since the loss of their settlement, had been tampering with the nabob to drive us out of the country (a manifest breach of their treaty) and we had reason to imagine he was well inclined, if that nation could lend him assistance, to accomplish it. It is true they were then in a low state, but a small force from Europe or their islands in India might have found employment for us on one side while the nabob, ready to seize such an opportunity, could have attacked us on the other. Therefore it was well worth our while to hazard much in order to place a prince on this throne whose interest thus would be connected with ours, and to drive him out who was not, nor ever likely to be, our friend.

CHAPTER EIGHT

Our scheme to overthrow the nabob was carried out with so little secrecy that the French got acquainted with it and seemed to rejoice in the thought that we were running to our own destruction. There was a small body of them—upwards of a hundred, collected from those that had made their escape from Chandernagore—at a small settlement of theirs near Kasimbazar. According to our agreement with the nabob, they should have quit his country. Though it can be imagined he never intended fulfilling that article, he had sent them so far—in order to remove them from our knowledge—that he could not recall them before we reached his capital. It is somewhat extraordinary that, notwithstanding the little care we took to keep our intentions a secret, yet they never came to the ear of the nabob or, if they did, he never gave credit to them until we set out. This was the state of affairs when we began our march on 13 June 1757.

Having the advantage of a river on our whole route, part of the army went by water, part by land. No kind of violence was offered to the inhabitants as we did not intend coming as conquerors but as deliverers. Nor did we receive the least hindrance or molestation from them. In this peaceful manner we pursued our march until the 18th when, being informed that the nabob had a pretty strong fort here called Cutwa, which commanded the river, a detachment of our regiment under the command of Captain [Eyre] Coote [who had in fact been promoted to the rank of major two days earlier] was sent to summon it to surrender or, in case of refusal, to use force. We had private information that the governor was in our interest and intended only making a show of resistance before retiring. This proved to be true, for, having fired the whole night of the 18th with no loss to our people, the garrison abandoned the fort in the morning of the 19th, leaving us masters of it. The same day the whole army joined the detachment.

Although the weather had favoured us, having had little rain at a time of year when much was expected, yet our people were greatly fatigued. It was therefore thought prudent to halt here a little, not only to rest the men, but likewise to see whether, now that we were within forty miles of the capital, our friend would openly manifest himself. On the 21st, the colonel assembled a Council of War at which he signified that from the last intelligence he was well convinced no country power would join us until by an action with the nabob we had determined things in our favour, and that he had called us together for our opinions whether or not we thought our strength was sufficient to proceed. A great majority of the council gave it as theirs that it was not. But on more maturely considering our situation, that the longer we deferred attacking the nabob the stronger he would grow, that our delays might perhaps give time to the French to join him, that the danger of retreat was greater than that of advancing—as those inhabitants who had been quiet spectators of our progress would, in order to justify themselves to their master, fall on us then—all these things weighed and considered, our proceeding was resolved on by the colonel notwithstanding the determination of the foregoing Council.

The city of Murshidabad is situated on a large island made by two branches of the Ganges. We had hitherto pursued our route on the opposite side but on 22 June, after the forementioned resolution, we crossed the river and advanced to our enemy with no impediment in the way to hinder our meeting. We made a forced march this day in order to reach a grove near which we were informed some of the nabob's army was encamped, but our intelligence was very vague and little to be depended on. It was twelve at night before the first division of the army arrived, having a rear of upwards of three miles in length, our men fatigued to the last degree. Altogether we were in such a situation as would have made us an easy prey to four hundred men of any spirit that dared to have attacked us. But the enemy we had to encounter were luckily not of that stamp.

On our arrival we had certain information that the nabob with his whole army was encamped within two miles of us. Picquets consisting of two captains and two hundred men were sent to take possession of a pleasure house belonging to him, called Plassey, situated about two hundred yards from the grove. This was done without meeting any opposition. Thus we remained all that night, the whole army lying on their arms.

The 23rd June about six o'clock in the morning, our spies brought us word that the nabob had drawn his army out of their camp and was moving towards us, on which the whole was ordered under arms. The Europeans from the time we set out had been divided into two battalions and were now drawn up accordingly, the first on the

right (in which was the detachment of our regiment) and
the second on the left. Each battalion was subdivided into
two grand divisions with an equal proportion of artillery,
and the sepoys were distributed on the right and on the
left. In this order we marched to that side of the grove
which faced a fine extensive plain. Our left was covered
by the house of Plassey, our rear by the grove. About four
hundred yards in our front was a pond, well banked and
apparently a post of strength, situated not very far from
the first entrenchment of the nabob's camp.

Scarcely were we drawn up when we received the fire
of the enemy's cannon, which killed two of the king's
grenadiers. On that we were ordered to retire into the
grove and cover ourselves behind a bank which surrounded it. The enemy soon took possession of the pond
in our front, from whence they plied us with grape and
kept a very warm and brisk fire on the grove with their
heavy artillery, consisting of thirty-two, twenty-four and
nine-pounders, but as we were sheltered behind the bank
it did little execution.

The plain seemed covered with their army, consisting
of horse, foot, some Europeans [French artillerymen]
whom we since learned numbered about fifty, elephants
and camels—affording us a grand, though terrible,
prospect. As they were drawn up, except for some few
advanced parties, at too great a distance for our short
sixes to do any execution, our hobit [howitzer] was advanced about two hundred yards in the front and fired
with success. But a party of horse made a movement as if
they intended to seize it and the men were ordered back
for fear of bringing on a general engagement—which at
that time was not thought expedient. However, from the
grove we returned their fire, which was very heavy and
would have annoyed us much but for the shelter we had
luckily found there. Their movements gave us reason to

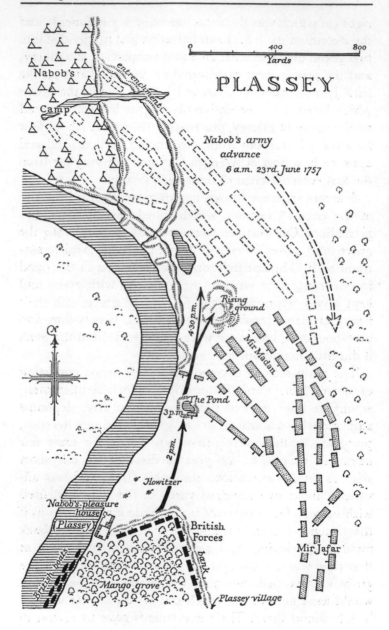

PLASSEY

0   400   800
Yards

Nabob's Camp

Nabob's army
advance
6 a.m. 23rd. June 1757

Rising
ground

4.30 p.m.

Mir Madan

The Pond
3 p.m.

2 p.m.

Howitzer

Nabob's pleasure
house
(Plassey)

British boats

British
Forces

Mango grove

bank

Plassey village

Mir Jafar

imagine that they intended surrounding us in order to make a general attack, and this seemed all the more likely when there fell a heavy shower of rain that might have been expected to render our firearms useless. But this was a case of our own apprehensions forming schemes for the enemy that they themselves never thought of.

At twelve o'clock it was reported that a party had attacked our boats and were destroying them. This sounded true, as it would then have been the most effectual thing they could have done to distress us, and might easily have been accomplished since the guard left to secure them was but small and they were about a quarter of a mile from the grove. The picquets of the night before were ordered to reinforce them but the report proved false and the orders were countermanded.

The enemy's fire now began to slacken and, shortly after, entirely ceased. In this situation we remained until two o'clock, when it was perceived that they were leaving the field, returning to their camp. Part were even in camp. The lucky moment was seized and the company of grenadiers belonging to the first battalion, with a couple of guns and some sepoys, were ordered to take possession of the pond which the enemy had held that morning. This was immediately executed without any loss, the enemy having quitted it some time before. Four platoons from the same battalion were ordered up to support them. Then the grenadiers with some sepoys were sent to take possession of a post about two hundred yards nearer the enemy's camp.

When we made these motions the enemy halted and immediately sent a strong party of horse towards our grove as if with intention to cut off the communication between our advanced parties and main body and took possession of a rising ground a little distance from the pond. These steps being the most prudent that they could have taken, we had just reason to expect a vigorous attack. We fired now with great success, they being within full reach of our cannon. At this period, orders were sent for the whole army to march out of the grove, but then it was considered that all our ammunition was there and that the enemy's party of horse seemed to be tending that way, so the orders were countermanded except for four platoons of the second battalion and two more guns. The enemy by this time had got some of their cannon to bear on us and plied us with small-arms fire from the first entrenchment of their camp as well as from their advanced party on the rising ground. But they had little effect, for our grenadiers' fire was so very warm as to prevent their returning it otherwise than in hurry and confusion, and their cannon were of little use, being large unwieldy pieces moved with great difficulty and most of them already lodged in their camp.

In this situation we remained about half an hour, when our cannon—which was very well served that day—seeming to have thrown them into some confusion and having, as we afterwards learned, killed their principal general [Mir Madan] and three or four of their elephants, the grenadiers with the platoons from the pond were ordered to drive the enemy from their advanced post on the rising ground. This was done with little danger, as they abandoned it as soon as it became clear we were making the attempt. From that moment they never more made head against us. We immediately pursued them into their camp and they as fast fled from it. Here we found most of their heavy cannon, some with upwards of a hundred oxen yoked to them, others dismounted, and all in the utmost confusion. That body of horse which had moved towards the grove in our first attempt, and on whom we still continued to fire, belonged, we were now informed, to our friend—being commanded by Mir Jafar. We had orders immediately to desist.

Our whole army now marched out of the grove and continued to pursue until five o'clock in the evening. Not having horse, this answered no other purpose than to keep up the panic which had made them so easy a conquest to our arms. This was manifest by the great confusion in which they fled, leaving all their cannon behind amounting to upwards of fifty pieces. According to their own account, they had above one hundred thousand fighting men in the field that day [in fact, about fifty thousand] of whom we killed and wounded about five hundred. Our loss was very inconsiderable, not above seventy [actually, 18 killed and 45 wounded]. We continued the pursuit to a small village about six miles from the field of battle, where we lay that night. Thus ended the battle of Plassey, which left us without obstacle masters of fulfilling our intentions.

On 24 June 1757, Colonel Clive had a meeting with Mir Jafar, who was saluted Nabob of Bengal and renewed his promise of fulfilling the articles of agreement. After that, he repaired to Murshidabad the capital, where he was publicly acknowledged.

Siraj-ud-daula, finding the battle going against him and one of his most skilful generals—the person he most relied on—being killed, had fled to Murshidabad where, taking out of his treasury what money and jewels he could conveniently carry off, his favourite woman, and a very small number of attendants, he pursued his way higher up the country. But to have let him escape would have proved of too much consequence and he was closely pursued, in the utmost distress, being plundered and abandoned by his people, overtaken, and made prisoner before the party of French who were coming to his aid could reach him. In this situation, it is said he showed the greatest abjectness of spirit, begging his life on any conditions from the son of the usurper. This not being granted, he was murdered on 4 July 1757 [when he was still only twenty years of age], agreeable to the policy of this despotic government. It was about a year since he had taken Calcutta, at which time he was the dread of all the Europeans settled there, and uncontrollable monarch of a great kingdom, at the head of a numerous and victorious army. Strange vicissitude of fortune! It strongly shows the consequence of allowing strangers to make settlements in a country any other way than as merchants, who ought always to be kept in a great state of dependence on the government that tolerates their residence, states being frequently so circumstanced—either through disaffection to their chief or opposition of parties—as to be exposed to the greatest revolutions by any power watchful for such opportunities or led to them by unforeseen circumstances. Thus chance or design equally expose them to danger through neglecting to keep foreigners in subjection. To chance (if such a thing there be) must be imputed the present revolution, for, if the nabob had chosen any other time to humble the insolence of the English, it is very probable he might have done it with security. Never before, and probably never again, will they be able to spare so considerable an armament from any of their settlements. Nothing less could have accomplished the revolution. Furthermore they had a chief to execute their designs, than whom a properer person could not possibly have been found, for Colonel Clive well knew from his experience in the country the spirit of these people, and how much a small number of Europeans with resolution could effect against them.

CHAPTER NINE

On 28 June our whole army marched into Kasimbazar
and the next day Colonel Clive, attended by a guard of
two captains, four subalterns and 160 men, proceeded to
Murshidabad, about five miles distant, where we arrived
the same day.

Here the first thing demanded and granted from the
new nabob was an augmentation of the gifts to be made to
the principals who had planned and executed the undertaking which gave him power, as well as to the governor
and council of Calcutta. Only afterwards was the fulfilling
of the rest of the articles of agreement relating to money
matters taken into consideration. It being found on examination that there was not near so much money in the
treasury as expected, and nothing like sufficient to accomplish all, it was resolved that but one half should be paid
at present and the remainder in three yearly payments. I
cannot help observing on the injustice of this decision, for
surely the terms originally stipulated ought first to have
been fulfilled; then, if anything remained, it might have
been distributed as an additional reward to the principals

and Calcutta council. Even had the commander only considered himself, no-one would have murmured. But in fact, the army and navy had very just reason to complain, to find themselves deprived of what was their right because of a posterior compact made in favour of many persons who little deserved it in any way other than in having been the primary cause of all the trouble, through their mismanagement and—without being too severe, I may say—the corruption of their former administration. But it is no less a melancholy than a true observation that self-interest—particularly where money is concerned— often blinds reason with imaginary advantages accruing therefrom, which are pursued at the expense of justice, at the expense of truth, thereby quitting the substance in pursuit of the shadow.

Money matters being for the present thus adjusted, the following treaty was confirmed.

TRANSLATE OF THE TREATY executed by Jaffer Ali Khan Bahauder [Mir Jafar]. In his own hand writing Viz.

In the presence of God and his Prophet I swear to abide by the terms of this agreement whilst I have life.

TREATY made with Admiral Watson, Colonel Clive, Governour Drake, Mr Watts, and the Committee.

1st The Agreement and Treaty made with Nabob Surajud Doulat I agree to and admit of.

2d The Enemies of the English are my enemies whether Europeans or others.

3d Whatever goods and Factories are belonging to the French in the provinces of Bengall, Bahaar [Bihar], and Orixa [Orissa], shall be delivered up to the English, and the French never permitted to have Factories or settlements more in those provinces.

4th To indemnify the Company for their losses by the capture of Calcutta, and the charge they have been at to repossess their Factories I will give One Crore of Rupees [*crore* = one hundred *lakhs*, i.e. ten million. Corneille notes that one rupee equalled two shillings and sixpence in the values of the time].

5th To indemnify the English Inhabitants who suffered by the capture of Calcutta I will give Fifty lacks [*lakhs*] of Rupees.

6th To indemnify the losses suffered by the Gentoes, Moors &c^a I will give twenty Lack of Rupees.

7th To indemnify the Armenian Riotts [*ryot*, farmer or cultivator, but here used to mean 'the poorer classes'. Corneille defines the Armenian *ryots* as 'English-protected persons'] of Calcutta who suffered by the capture of Calcutta, I will give seven lacks of Rupees. The division of those donations to be left to the Admiral, the Colonel and the Committee.

8th The Lands within the Moratta ditch all round Calcutta, which are now possessed by other Zemidars, and Six hundred Yards all round without the ditch I will give up entirely to the Company.

9th The Zemidary [landlord's rights] of the Land to the Southward of Calcutta as low as Culpei [Kalpi] shall be in the hands of the English Company, and under their Government and orders; the Customary Rents of every district within that tract to be paid by the English into the King's Treasury.

10th Whenever I send for the Assistance of the English Troops their pay and charges shall be disbursed by me.

11th From Hughly downwards I will build no new Forts near the River.

12th As soon as I am established Suba of the three

I

Provinces I will immediately perform the above
mentioned articles.

Dated the 5th of the Month Ramazan in the fourth
Year of the present Reign. [Signed first in early June
1757]

Besides the foregoing treaty there was another in which
was mentioned a donation of fifty lakhs of rupees to be
divided between the army and navy, and several other
very considerable ones. The latter, as mentioned before,
were inserted after the work was done, whereas that to
the military and navy was agreed on before we left
Chandernagore.

As we had no precedent for such a gift falling to the
land army, it was therefore necessary to settle the proportion that each rank ought to receive. This certainly should
have been done before we set out on the expedition,
when the prospect of money being but distant would have
given justice a fairer play. But our hopes of success
seemed then too great a chimera for us seriously to take
into consideration the question of dividing the spoil. That
it might be done with as much equality as possible, the
colonel ordered a Council of War consisting of an equal
proportion of officers from each corps and each rank. But
some days before it met, a report prevailing that but half
the money stipulated for the army and navy was then to
be paid, and the rest in three yearly payments, the following letter was written in order that it might be presented
to the colonel before the sitting.

Sir—

As from experience and observation the Officers under
your command have always found you willing and ready
to serve them, and it being reported that but one half of

the money which was stipulated for the Army on the accomplishment of the Service which is now done, is at present to be paid, the remainder on security payable in three Years, We therefore beg leave to lay before you some considerations in regard to that, which the inevitable hurry of business that you must at present be involved in may have occasioned to escape your observation.

If the case is agreeable to report, that half which is payable in Three Years, or even in a much less time, can be of little or no advantage to most on this expedition; for allowing it to meet with no obstacle in the payment, our several duties will undoubtedly long before the expiration of that time disperse us into different parts of the World, by which means it will be almost impossible to transact that affair; but on the other hand if the payment should admitt of any difficulty, though we as a collective body are of some little weight, dispersed we dwindle to nothing and cannot in that situation inforce anything. The case cannot admitt of those difficulties in regard to the Company, for by your means their affairs are settled on a stronger foundation than ever, and therefore by keeping up a sufficient Force here they will always be able to make good any security which the Nabob at present can give them.

In this perhaps We may appear to be a little too sanguine, as even half the money promised is a great sum to men in our situations. True, Sir. But the promise which was made us at setting out, joined to the success which our arms have met with, has led us to the flattering idea of gaining considerable advantages. Such an event has not ever happened, nor probably will ever again. Consider this, Sir, and that now you have in power what few men have had: making a number happy. You will do it we are all convinced, if consisting with your constant rule of acting, Equity and Justice. We therefore will add nothing more than that

We are—
Sir &c^{as} &c^{as}—

Muxidavad
the 3rd July 1757

This letter was approved by all the officers, but when it was offered to be signed a difficulty was started by Captain Grant, who refused to put his name unless he could put it as Major (he having acted as such from the first of the expedition). This the other officers refused, as they did not intend he should share as such. So the letter remained unsigned. Nevertheless it was presented to the colonel, who told us in answer that it was true that there was but half the money then to be paid. He said that on examination of the treasury it was not found sufficient to answer the whole, that therefore he thought it but justice that each body should receive an equal proportion of what was promised, that he was a Company's servant and would deservedly lay himself open to censure did he—to the Company's prejudice—pay the army and navy the whole sum stipulated. He added that, if we pleased, he would negotiate the present payment of the other half with the merchants, in the best and most advantageous manner he could for our interest.

After this the Council of War sat, and everything was seemingly settled to the satisfaction of all. But all the members were dining that day with the colonel, and some objections arose after dinner concerning one of the articles, viz: 'Whether the money should be paid to the troops at Kasimbazar, or sent down to Calcutta in order to be sorted?'—for it consisted of rupees of different values. It had been carried in the morning by a great majority that it should be sent down. The colonel, thinking that gentlemen could not so soon recede from their opinion, now quite irregularly put the question a second time to the vote, when it was carried in a great majority for the negative! Perceiving the consequences of such a step—that the navy [which could witness the sorting at Calcutta, but not at Kasimbazar] might justly think we had not acted candidly with them—the colonel took upon him of his own authority to have it sent down none the less, and had the question struck out of the Council minutes. In this, though it was a necessary act of despotism, he met with disagreeable scenes from some officers which, joined to the immoderate donations given to many undeserving persons, contributed to lessen the esteem they had for their commander and was productive of much uneasiness to him afterwards.

The minutes of the Council of War stood then as follows

COPY OF A COUNCIL OF WAR held at Muxidavad the 3rd July 1757—

Present
Robert Clive Esqr &c^a PRESIDENT

MAJORS
James Kilpatrick
Archibald Grant
Eyre Coote

FROM THE KING'S DETACHMT
Capt John Corneille
Lieut Joseph Adnett
Lieut Martin Yorke

FROM THE BENGAL DETACHMT
Capt Alix Grant
Lieut Archd Keir
Ensn—Champion

FROM THE MADRAS DETACHMT

Capt Robert Campbell
Lieut Bryan Scotney
Ensn—Stringer

FROM THE BOMBAY DETACHMT

Capt Andw Armstrong
Lieut Villars Walsh
Ensn—Robinson

OF THE ARTILLERY

Capt—Pashaud
Lieut Thoms Lewis
Lieut—Kinch

There being no regulation among the land forces on this expedition, for the division of plunder, or booty taken from the enemy, or for the gift made by the Nabob, this Council of War consisting of the Field Officers of the Army, and of three officers chosen by each respective detachment is assembled to settle the same. After thorough consideration of the matter, It is agreed.

That every thing shall be determined in this Council of War by the Majority of Votes.

That One Eighth part of the amount of the whole booty and gift be paid to the Commander in Chief and Major James Kilpatrick: that is to say two thirds of the Eighth to the Commander in Chief, and One third to Major James Kilpatrick.

That four Eighths be paid to the Captains, Staff Officers, and Subalterns in such manner that the share of every Captain and Staff Officer shall be double to that of a Subaltern. The Staff Officers here meant are the Aid de Camp, Secretary, Judge Advocate, Pay master, the Commissary on the Fort St George establishment, the Commissary on the Bengal establishment, and the Commissary of Artillery. It is also meant that the Chaplain, Surgeons, Quarter-Masters, shall share as Subalterns.

That One Eighth and a half, or three Sixteenths, be paid to Volunteers, Non Commissioned Officers, Soldiers, Artificers &cᵃ in the following proportion:

To each Volunteer, Surgeon's Mate, Conductor of the Train, Serjeant Majors, Quarter Master Serjᵗˢ, Three times the share of an European private Sentinel.

To each Serjeant twice as much as a private Sentinel.

To each Corporal, Bombardier, European Drum, and Artificer half a share more than a private Sentinel.

To each Gunner, Matross [apprentice gunner], and Mustee [half-caste] Sentinel, the same as an European private Sentinel.

To each Topaz [dark-skinned half-caste of Indo-Portuguese descent] and Black drum two thirds of the share of an European private Sentinel, the surplus third to be thrown into the three sixteenths.

That One Eighth be paid to the Seapoys, the Lascars (a kind of porter) in the following proportions:

To Keysar Sing the Commandant of the Madras Seapoys, and the Commandant of the Bengal Seapoys, One Sixteenth part of the Eighth to be shared equally between them, the latter to share from the date of his appointment.

To the Subahdars (Captains of Seapoys) excluding Keysar Sing and the Commandant of the Bengal Seapoys, three Sixteenths.

To the Jemmadars (Subalterns) of the Seapoys and the Serangs (chiefs of the porters) of the Lascars four Sixteenths.

To the Havildars, Naigues [naiks], and Colour men of the Seapoys, and Tindals of the Lascars (all being kinds of non-commissioned Officers), all sharing equally two sixteenths.

To the Tom Toms (drummers), Trumpeters, and

private Seapoys and the Lascars, all sharing equally six sixteenths.

One sixteenth of the whole plunder still remaining undivided, It is agreed that out of it the share of Major Archibald Grant (commanding the Detachment of his Majesty's 39th Regiment) be made equal to half the amount of Major James Kilpatrick's share, and that the rest of the sixteenth be thrown into the share of the Captains, Staff Officers, and Subalterns in consideration of the many staff Officers who divide as Captains.

It is agreed that the detachment which did arrive on the *Cumberland* do share in the plunder taken from the French at Chandernagore, in consideration of that Ship being then in the river; but that the plunder taken from the Moors at Hughly, Calcutta, Bougie Bougie [Budge Budge], &cᵃ be only shared amongst the troops arrived at the time of those captures.

It is agreed that the Officers and Sailors belonging to the Squadron which came with the Army on the expedition to Muxidavad are not to receive prize money with the Military.

It is further agreed that no person shall share in two capacities, that whoever shall be killed or die during a Siege or action, his share of the prize money acquired by such siege or action, shall be paid to his executors or agents. That Officers succeeding others killed during a siege or action shall be entitled only to the share due his former post. That the prize money belonging to non-commissioned Officers and soldiers be paid to their respective Captains, and that the Agents for the Captors be allowed to draw 5 pʳ Cent on the sale of all goods, and one pʳ Cᵗ on all money taken. That Jewels and plate are to have commission drawn but as for money.

It is unanimously desired that Colonel Clive shall negotiate for prompt payment with the Nabob, Juger

Said—one of the principal merchants of the East, reckoned worth some millions of money [probably Jagat Seth, the great banker]—or others, in the best manner he is able.

Given under our hands
this 3^d day of July 1757

(N.B. The sixteenth which, in the foregoing Council of War, was given to Major Grant and the rest of the officers, was later altered and given first to the officers and then, when it was found that there was a great disproportion between the prize money given to ordinary sailors and soldiers, entirely given to the latter.)

Subsequent proceedings having angered the spirit of most of the officers, they now refused to sign, saying that as the colonel had broken through the first article they did not think themselves bound to observe any, that some of the terms had been agreed to entirely out of complaisance to him and that they now wished these to be altered—in particular that concerning Captain Grant, who had no more right to an extraordinary share than Captain Coote (both having acted as majors). They therefore desired another sitting to have these affairs settled.

In order to pacify them, the colonel so far gave way to their opposition as to alter that article concerning Captain Grant and add that whole sixteenth to the officers' share (which was afterwards disposed of as above mentioned). This seemed to appease them. But the minute could not yet be signed as some members, during the foregoing transactions, had been sent with a detachment to Patna.

It may seem somewhat extraordinary that those gentlemen who acted as majors should not receive prize money agreeable to their rank, but as neither the colonel nor the governor nor council were in truth invested with power to confer any commission higher than that of captain, it was thought unreasonable that those gentlemen should share —only from a nominal appointment—in a way that would much lessen the proportion of the rest. In any event, Captain Grant had no reason to complain, having been considered in the extraordinary gifts and receiving, for his portion, a *lakh* of rupees, or upwards of twelve thousand pounds sterling. Judge therefore what sums must have been spent that way.

During these transactions, a detachment under the command of Captain Coote was sent in pursuit of those French—in number about 120—who had come down in order to assist Siraj-ud-daula. They left Murshidabad on 6 July and followed as far as Patna but without success, the French having got notice of their being pursued in time enough to get out of the nabob's provinces before they could be overtaken.

The 11th of this month we received the first account of the loss of Vizagapatam, which the French became masters of on 25 June 1757. As I mentioned before, it was a place not defensible, and the additional number of men which our ship had left there could not possibly answer any other end than to make the conquest of much more consequence to the French. They, it seems, were loath to commence hostilities from a consciousness, I presume, of our superior strength in India. But as soon as we had begun by the reduction of Chandernagore, Mr Bussy marched his army towards our settlements and dispossessed us of all our holdings in the kingdom of Golconda. The gentleman who was chief of the place at that time vaunted, ere the French came down, that he would defend it, but on their appearance his martial spirit vanished—not leaving him even presence of mind sufficient to make a good retreat. He would have had a fine opportunity for making a good retreat, one of the Company's ships being in the road which could have carried off the whole garrison with great ease. In lieu of that, trunks, tables and chairs were all that was saved. On the Frenchman's preparation to raise a battery, they capitulated without so much as firing one shot.

On the death of Siraj-ud-daula, most of the zemindars and men of consequence in the province of Bengal, being thereby absolved from the oath which they had all taken at his accession, seemed reconciled to the revolution and according to custom swore allegiance to the present family. Probably the presence of the colonel and the vicinity of the army contributed a good deal to the peaceful state of affairs. Matters being now in so fair a way of being settled, the colonel took that opportunity of going down to Calcutta, leaving one of the Council and some other gentlemen to finish all business. On 6 August he left Murshidabad. On his arrival at Calcutta, thinking it necessary to have part of the army near that settlement, he ordered down the king's detachment and some of the Company troops. Accordingly, we left Kasimbazar on the 20th for that purpose and arrived at the quarters designated for our men, at Chandernagore, on the 23rd.

On our passage we heard of Admiral Watson's death, which had happened on the day we left Kasimbazar. Thus did this gentleman, after having met with success in all his undertakings and having thereby accumulated a very considerable fortune, fall victim to the climate of Bengal. He was much regretted by all his people, and with justice, being esteemed a man of great honesty, great disinterestedness, and a spirit not to be biassed from the pursuit of what he thought touched the honour and advantage of his country. He was succeeded in the command by Admiral Pocock.

The colonel, on his arrival in Calcutta, far from meeting with that reception which his successes had promised, found the spirits there much exasperated in regard to money matters, the navy in particular. Admiral Watson had been appointed to the committee in Calcutta but had always refused to sit as a member, and the committee made this a handle to exclude him in the partition of the donation allotted to them. This fact, joined with the prevailing notion that it was the colonel who had principally prevented the forces receiving the whole of the agreed booty at once, induced both the navy and army to show him all possible signs of dislike. On 29 August he again returned to Murshidabad, promising he would try all in his power to get the whole for the army and the navy. In his absence the murmurs and disaffection still increased, and his return to Calcutta on 17 September—without having been successful—brought them to such a height as obliged the governor and Council to offer to buy the twelve-and-a-half lakhs of rupees due from the nabob over three years for a sum of ten lakhs paid forthwith. With some difficulty this proposition was made heard, but it was at last accepted and calm again restored. Had the colonel, on his first arrival at Murshidabad, made that offer (which was certainly in his power) it would have been received with alacrity and the merit would have accrued solely to him. He would thus have gained the affections of his officers and men and saved himself much uneasiness, without putting the Company to any more expense than they now were at. Whereas by the way the grant was made he reaped no advantage, nay, the reverse, for it appeared that he who should particularly have exerted himself for the interest of the army was almost the only one who thought their demand unjust and opposed it. Admiral Watson got his proportion of the committee money which amounted to three *lakhs* of rupees.

After adjusting this affair, it was found on examination that, according to the division of prize money agreed in the Council of War, the private soldiers would receive much short of what the sailors did. In order to rectify this and bring them on equality, most of the officers were assembled and, as taken notice of before, gave up unanimously for that purpose the sixteenth that had been thrown into their share. This not yet being sufficient, Colonel Clive and Major Kilpatrick promised to make up the remainder out of their pockets. This was but a promise and was not executed at least at the time I left Bengal, nor probably ever will be, for the latter gentleman died shortly after. In him the Company lost a good officer and faithful servant, whose merit solely had raised him from a very low station to the rank he then held and in which—purely from the dint of strong natural parts and sound judgement—he behaved to the satisfaction of all and on many occasions showed a great military genius, being cool in danger, even in the greatest possessing a presence of mind which did not let him miss the least advantage that might be taken. He was greatly loved by the soldiers, making it his business always to see them done justice to and, as far as circumstances allowed, supplied with necessities. This gentleman was almost the only man left of that detachment which had first come to the relief of Calcutta. He left a fortune of upwards of sixty thousand pounds sterling, much inferior to what many others had collected on this occasion, particularly as he was one considered in the private donations from which alone arose the real advantages. The proportion of the first stipulated gift of the nabob's and the prize money taken at Chandernagore amounted, for a captain, only to near three thousand pounds, and for the private men, about fifty, which though considerable was yet, comparatively speaking, trifling.

CHAPTER TEN

On 27 August we received the first account of the regiment's being ordered home, by the arrival of one of our officers from the coast. But as Captain Grant had no letter from Colonel Adlercron to that effect, our joy on the occasion was much damped. Our situation then was truly disagreeable. It was certain that the colonel had received such an order, and yet there were no directions from him, which gave us just room to apprehend that our detachment would have to stay in India long after the rest of the regiment had gone. This was particularly likely as current rumours from the north made it probable that it would be necessary for the army shortly to march that way.

At the beginning of November, hearing of disturbances in some of his distant provinces, the new nabob took the field, at the same time acquainting Colonel Clive with his intention and desiring to be joined by him and the Europeans. This request was considered and, though it appeared to some that the security of Calcutta required the army's stay, it was granted.

The king's troops had always behaved remarkably well and may justly be allowed to have contributed not a little to the success of the English arms. From this, it may be presumed, arose the many singular marks of esteem and regard which Colonel Clive on many occasions showed them. This was particularly manifest now by the great desire he expressed to have them with him on this expedition, little expecting to meet with reluctance from those who had always been the first to support his intentions. But the state of affairs at this time made their attitude otherwise.

From the time of our return to Chandernagore, our men had begun to be very sickly, and the excesses which their prize money furnished them with the means of gratifying, the badness of the climate at this time of year, as well as the very inactive state they were allowed to remain in, all joined to sweep them off by dozens a day. In a short time our numbers were reduced from about 270 men to 120, and even those poor remains were so worn down and weak as to be unfit for any kind of service for many months. The news of our being ordered home seemed to revive their drooping spirits, but these were greatly damped again by the uncertainty of the time of its being put in execution.

Thus was this poor shattered detachment situated when Colonel Clive again proposed taking the field. In order to prepare things for this second campaign, the troops were ordered to encamp near Chandernagore. This was done on 10 November 1757. Our dilemma was now very great. By going up the country, we would certainly prolong our stay for six months, perhaps twelve—for if the order came after our departure, we either would be too far distant to return in time to go with the ships then in the river, or else, probably, engaged in such a service as in honour we could not quit. On the other hand, the great inclination the colonel showed to have us, as well as the obligation some (nay, may I say the whole) were under to him, laid us open to the imputation of ingratitude if we made any objection to attending him on this occasion.

Thus were we circumstanced when Captain Grant received an order from the admiral to repair with the detachment under his command to Calcutta, in order that the men might be distributed on board his Majesty's ships as the service then required. I must observe that, from the time of our landing, the admiral had retained the power of recalling us at his pleasure. This order, when shown to Colonel Clive, seemed to surprise and disappoint him. However, he immediately wrote to Mr Pocock, who shortly after sent a second letter to Captain Grant signifying that he required but one officer of each rank and the men; the rest of the officers, if they chose, might attend the colonel on the proposed expedition. This increased our dilemma, as the fact of its being left to our choice exposed us to being superseded in rank if we were detained in the country any time after the rest of the regiment. This particularly affected me, who was then eldest lieutenant.

Captain Grant therefore resolved to represent the affair to the colonel in its proper light. It was received by him with a good deal of emotion and dissatisfaction, but he told us we might act as we pleased and were at liberty to pursue our inclinations. This spoke with a countenance that plainly showed he was much disappointed and vexed. The mortification which some of us felt at being the occasion of his uneasiness (which was certainly paying us the highest compliment) determined us to run the chance of attending him if only he would make it an order, so as to give us some plea in case of our being superseded. But no. He would have our service without compulsion or not at all.

We were ordered to leave camp and return to Chander-nagore, which we did, with about twelve men fit for service out of the poor remains of the detachment, the fatigue of only four days' encampment having reduced us thus low. Our departure was manifestly much to the satis-faction of the Company's officers, for the distinction which the colonel on all occasions showed our corps had brought them to look on us with a jealous eye and had been one of the primary causes of the great dislike they had latterly shown the colonel. The rest of the army set out for Kasimbazar on the 16th.

The great desire the colonel had shown to have us with him, in my opinion adding greatly to the many obliga-tions I in particular had on all occasions received from him, left a sting in my bosom that on cool reflection made me very uneasy. I now began to fear I had but too much laid myself open to the imputation of ingratitude, a vice that of all others seems to me of the blackest dye. Thus to remain long was a situation not to be borne and after mature reflection I could think of nothing that would more effectually restore calm again than to acknowledge my error to the colonel. For this purpose I wrote him the following letter.

Sir,
    Notwithstanding my conduct at present may justly expose me to the imputation of great unsteadiness in my resolutions, yet I would lay myself open to that and worse to clear as much as in my power the charge of ingratitude to You, Sir, from whom I shall always acknowledge to have received great obligation. It's a charge which I now first begin to fear I have but too much deserved; and though I am sensible nothing in my power can make amends for my late behaviour, not even the offer of my service which would but expose me to a mortifying

K

refusal; Yet I find no other way to banish that uneasiness of mind which I at present lie under.—Believe me sincere then Sir when I assure you I am sorry for what has passed; and thoroughly convinced of my error, am willing and ready if you think my service worth accepting of following you on this expedition. I know the answer I am exposed to in return for my late conduct, but am easy from the knowledge of the person I write to, for whom permit me to add no one can have a greater esteem than

Sir

&c^a J: C

Chandernagore

the 20th November 1757

The 3rd December I received the following answer.

Sir,

Where was the necessity of vindicating your conduct to one who is fully convinced Captain Corneille is incapable of acting wrong through principle? I know ingratitude to be as far from your way of thinking as want of friendship is from mine. Indeed the want of the Kings Officers upon the present expedition has occasioned me many tormenting reflections and I must esteem it a great misfortune I could not have the Company and Assistance of those through choice, on whom I very much depended.

I need not tell you what satisfaction your accompanying me on the present expedition would afford, but I much fear it would occasion a renewal of the late dissatisfactions, and consequently be the means of great uneasiness to myself, and of disservice to the Company's affairs, which at present require much attention.

Present my best wishes to your Brother Officers and

believe that your merit will always entitle you to the
Esteem of

Sir

Muxidavad &c^a

the 28th Novr 1757 R. Clive

Thus ended an affair which gave me greater uneasiness than I have often experienced. I have been the more
particular in relating every circumstance, not only to
show a very amiable part of Colonel Clive's character, his
readiness to forgive, which quality he possesses in an
eminent degree; but likewise that you may, with that
sound judgement of which you are master, confirm me
blameless or censure me if otherwise.

In the interim between my writing the foregoing letter
and receiving an answer, Captain Grant at last got the
much expected order from Colonel Adlercron, by which
he was to leave what officers and men chose to remain in
the Company's service and, with the remainder, return to
Europe in the best and most expeditious manner that the
governor could assist him in.

There being then in the river three ships intended for
Europe, these were ordered to take us on board. The
officers drawing for places, the *Marlborough*—the first to
sail—fell to my lot. We sailed from the Balasore road on
the much desired but very little expected voyage home;
not even a gleam of hope had I of such an event since
leaving Ireland, until I heard of the order; nor even then
could I give credit to it, being unable to account for what
possibly could have occasioned recall at a time when the
Company's affairs in India seemed to require our presence
much more than on our arrival.

Some days before we embarked, the intelligence from
Colonel Clive's expedition signified that all affairs were in
a fair way of being amicably made up. His name being,

in those parts, of as much consequence as an army, contributed a good deal towards bringing the powerful and turbulent to reason without blows. Well was it for the Company that affairs took that turn, as the situation in Calcutta seemed to require the presence of the army. There they had, by neglect, allowed the greatest part of the French prisoners taken at Chandernagore to escape, and they, it was said, lay lurking about that part of the country to the number of two hundred, watching for the departure of the fleet so that they could plunder the town. Parties had been sent out in search of them, but to no effect. The garrison being very small, it was thought by the English that the admiral would determine to remain there until the arrival of a reinforcement from up the country.

Thus did this government, through their bad administration, expose themselves to imminent danger. Not satisfied with that, in another instance of still more glaring misconduct, they gave an opportunity of spreading the influence of their neglect even to the coast. The French officers had at first been permitted to reside on their parole at Chinsurah, the Dutch settlement, but, finding that they there carried on a correspondence up the country to our detriment, we removed them to Chandernagore in order that they might be more closely observed. Here, still, it was thought they were too much at hand to second the attempts which it was probable their nation would make to recover their losses in Bengal, so it was determined to send the greatest part of them to Madras. But instead of doing it at a proper season and with a sufficient guard to prevent their escaping, they were sent when navigation was dangerous and on board a ship which partly belonged to the governor and was said to be insured for much more than its value. It was navigated by black men, except for three Europeans, one of whom—

the captain—returned to Calcutta before the ship sailed and left her command to the mate. All this took place notwithstanding the fact that the French had been quite open in their declaration, saying publicly that they did not think themselves in any way bound by the articles of capitulation as we had manifestly broke through them in many instances. They had intimated that they would put into execution what they in fact did shortly after setting sail, which was to make themselves masters of the ship. They took her in to Mussulapatnam [Masulipatam], a settlement of theirs on the coast of Coromandel.

This, though a most manifest neglect and fraud, was but of a piece with the accounts given of the administration of the Company long before the commencement of the trouble, and strongly attests their veracity. Had the Company's conduct since the late calamities run counter to those reports, the good-natured part of mankind might have thought that envy and prejudice had had a hand in assigning, to their prejudice, causes productive of the late dire effects which really were not true, or exaggerated as a result of the distress and damages suffered on that occasion. But they disdained to appear what they were not, nor ever had been, preferring uniformity of conduct and a continuance in their old beaten path. Conscious or fearful of soon losing that power they had made so bad use of, they were desirous of laying up a store against the impending storm. Little regarding the means, so they accomplished the end.

I have now, my dear Father, insensibly spun out what at first I thought would be contained in a few sheets to almost a volume. So glib runs the pen when prompted by duty and inclination! If you have found me diffuse and tedious in my foregoing narrative, I take shelter under my motive from the blame I otherwise would justly deserve; and should that be the case, I beg you will read no further but burn the sheets. But if I have been so happy as to have contributed in the least to your amusement, I may then hope that the following observations will not be less entertaining.

CHAPTER ELEVEN

Great is the scope that a contemplative man would find were he to make observations in the province of Bengal. As it is extensive, however, it would require time and a knowledge of the language to make them fully satisfactory. I know that, from the want of both requisites, what follows is but very superficial, although it will serve as a proof that I did not pass through the novelties of this distant world with an entirely inactive mind; that I made, though little, yet some small use of that faculty without the exertion of which the chimney corner will yield as much improvement as traversing the most distant region. I must take notice that, where there is a resemblance between the customs and manners of these people and those on the coast of Coromandel, I omit mentioning them. And some things which were there forgot I have particularised here.

The province of Bengal has deservedly acquired the epithet of rich, for very few countries in the known world can compare with it for goodness of soil, variety and abundance of manufacture, greatness of rivers, and number of inhabitants. Were it not for the unhealthiness of its climate (which, it must be observed, is remarkably so only to Europeans) and the badness of its government—two great ingredients towards the happiness of life—it would be a desirable part of the world to reside in.

That the air of Bengal at particular seasons is somewhat malignant, every one who lies exposed at those times to the dews can sufficiently experience; but the natives, from whom the healthiness or unhealthiness of a climate can justly be judged, live here to as great an age as in most other countries, and are as free from disorders. To strangers, without care, it is very fatal. This our detachment only too severely experienced after their return from Murshidabad, when we lost in the space of two months one third of our people. This ought not, however, to be entirely imputed to the place, but rather to the affluence of money which gave them the means of indulging passions much more destructive than the worst of climates.

Great are the vicissitudes of heat and cold, yet they come on by a gradual transition. May, in my opinion, is as hot as human nature can well support. June, July and August, which form the rainy season and are subject to great thunder and lightning, are very warm, yet frequently each day is refreshed by heavy cooling showers. September and October are fine but still very hot. Though November, December, January and February are in the morning liable to thick fogs and very cold, in the middle of the day they are as delightfully temperate as even an European constitution would desire. After that the heat gradually increases.

The first setting-in of the cold is generally the time of the sickly season, which is imputed to the filth that the subsided waters leave on the land. The higher one advances up the country the more healthy it is. But the parts about the European settlements being flat and full of marshes and woods, it is no way surprising that fevers and fluxes—so particular to such situations—should be rife. Those who are attacked with these disorders are soon hurried off. If they get the better of them, they do not recover until the returning sun. About the latter end of February begin what are called the north-easters, which continue until May. These are terrible squalls of wind, rain and thunder which help to purify the air and clear away the malignant vapours. Notwithstanding the difficulty of divesting oneself of partiality to one's native clime, yet I think that this —as most in India—is preferable to ours for the majority of inhabitants. They, being always of the lower class, can with much greater ease guard against the inclemency of heat than of cold. How many poor wretches in our northern regions suffer great hardships from the rigour of our seasons; but here, where the all-enlivening sun is felt throughout the year, food is almost all the poorer kind have to labour for. How happy ought they to be whose chief want is so amply supplied! So much so that no part of the known world can compare with this for fruitfulness. The luxuriancy of its soil is such as to yield in most places three crops a year, consisting of rice and all grains particular to the East, with the addition of wheat and peas, both in so great abundance as to supply all the European settlements in India. The ground is in every part covered with fine pasture, showing plenty and beauty spread with a liberal hand over tracts where tyranny and oppression lord it without control. All kind of trees which the coast produces thrive in Bengal, and many more. Fruits are the same, and in much greater perfection—particularly the mango which here excels any thing in that way that our part of the world affords.

Among the many advantages which this country is blessed with, its rivers are the most considerable. All proceed from that remarkable one called the Ganges which, even four hundred miles from its discharge in the sea, still measures near a league across. It branches out into innumerable rivers, taking different names according to the countries and principal towns it passes through, many of which are, notwithstanding the long continuance of the European settlements, very little known to them. It has different outlets into the sea, some of them, by account, much more considerable than that which runs by Calcutta, and which is called the Hugli river after a considerable Moorish town of that name. The Hugli river is, at its discharge, four leagues over and navigable two hundred miles up for a sixty-gun ship. All the other branches are the same for large boats, which facilitates trade and contributes to the riches which are so remarkable here. For by means of the river, the most distant provinces can supply each other at a cheap rate with those necessaries which they may want, and can convey their manufactures to the principal mart.

Though the Ganges is a large and deep river, yet the rapidity of its current and tide, which runs at the rate of nine miles an hour, and the many banks of sand which it abounds with, particularly at its entrance, makes navigation extremely dangerous. To obviate these difficulties as much as possible, each European nation has pilots at fixed salaries who, by long experience and constant practice, become thoroughly acquainted with all its sands. They also have fixed buoys on the principal sands. Large ships are generally obliged to navigate stern foremost, dragging an anchor, as the channels in some parts are not much more than twice the breadth of a ship and the banks are steep on each side. If they touched the banks it would certainly overset them. Notwithstanding all these precautions, ships are frequently lost. What will not the desire of gain prompt men to! All difficulties vanish before it, and without that spur many things which now are practised would scarce be attempted.

Most European nations have settlements on this branch of the river but are far exceeded by the English at Calcutta, by reason of the spirit of their trade, the extent of the town, and the stateliness of the buildings. Calcutta was somewhat checked by the devastation committed by the Moors, but now begins to recover and enters again into that splendour, magnificence and luxury that the Company's merchants were always famous for, seemingly already forgetful of those incredible hardships which their insolence and imprudence so lately involved them in.

They have planned out a considerable fortification about a mile from where the town now stands, as being a situation which commands more of the river, but they go on so slowly with the execution that I believe it will be of little service to them for many years. Their old fort, called Fort William, is a very slight square, which was badly garrisoned and destitute of everything to make it capable of defence when attacked by the Moors. Mark, however, the genius of this settlement. In their indefensible town they had a most magnificent palace for the president, with a ballroom reckoned the largest and most completely finished of any in India—the whole of which the Moors destroyed out of their hatred for the then government, erecting out of its ruins, while they were masters of the place, a mosque. The English, to add to the weakness of the settlement, had permitted houses to be built almost touching the wall, from whence, at the time of the siege, they received the most hurt. In short, pleasure was their pursuit, though this did not prevent them from carrying on a most flourishing trade infinitely beyond either the Dutch or the French.

The Dutch have a settlement called Chinsurah, situated about forty miles higher up the river, where there is a small square fort of very little strength. This place almost joins Hugli, one of the most considerable Moorish trading towns in these parts, which the English plundered and almost entirely demolished in retaliation for Calcutta. In this place, Eastern luxury was carried to a great height for, being enriched by their trade and thereby supplied with the produce of most parts of the world, they could give full scope to that disposition for which they are deservedly remarkable. They now have it back in their possession and are repairing, with great expedition, the damages they lately suffered.

About two miles on the Calcutta side of Chinsurah, the French had their settlement called Chandernagore, where there was a tolerably good square fort, very well provided with all kinds of warlike stores, which rendered it a place scarce able to be taken by any country power although it proved insufficient against a European, as they discovered when Admiral Watson and Colonel Clive attacked it. It is now entirely demolished, as are most of the houses, of which there were many, some of them very good. I cannot help here observing the different policy of the two nations. Chandernagore, when attacked by what was for those parts a considerable fleet and a pretty numerous army consisting of near four thousand whites and blacks, made a brave and good defence. Calcutta, when attacked only by Moors—people inexperienced in that particular branch of war—shortly fell, being unprovided with everything, even in a settlement which infinitely surpassed the other both in riches and trade. Surely so many repeated instances of neglect will at last awake them from their long-continued lethargy.

The balance of trade which all the European nations carry on in Bengal is entirely in its favour, the exchange for their commodities being mostly money. The principal thing we get from thence is saltpetre, besides which there are great quantities of muslins of various kinds and names, and silk manufactured in different manners. There are also gum lac, opium, all kinds of grain in the greatest abundance, and many other things for almost all the markets in the world. Bengal has always been remarkable for the great cheapness, variety and fineness of needle work, in thread, in gold, silver, and coloured silks, most of which I suppose have been introduced since the first settlement of the Europeans, as all their patterns are of that taste. These things are done by men, women, and children in their leisure hours, and are sold a third cheaper than could possibly be afforded in our country, owing to the number of inhabitants and the great plenty of grain, which is almost all they want and indeed, little as it is, almost all they are allowed to have. This is a natural consequence of Eastern government, where despotism and its attendant tyrannic slavery mar the best gifts of nature, which here would produce—if there were liberty and good laws—plenty, ease and happiness.

The original inhabitants of this country were Gentoo idolaters, distinguished by their different castes. But at present the country is, as it has been for many years, in the hands of the Moors, and where they reign despotism prevails. Bengal is ruled by a governor, commonly called nabob, appointed by the Mughal, under whom he rules a tract of land of very great extent. The power and riches of these nabobs generally render them independent of their masters and they have frequently beaten armies sent to collect their tribute.

Laws are not to be sought for here, for they have none but the will of their superior, who rules as caprice, capacity or passion guides. The fruit of this is seldom that which all princes ought to be desirous of—the love of their subjects. Indeed, they never expect it, and therefore in the fine weather take the field with a considerable army, sometimes to encounter enemies, but always to collect the dues and tributes. Without such display of power, the dues would scarce be paid.

In governments of this kind, suspicion and mistrust are frequent and are commonly wiped out by murder, a policy that seems as natural to this kind of constitution as clemency does to ours. Riches are frequently the cause of their great men's destruction for, as they generally stick at nothing to collect them, subjects of complaint are never wanting sufficient to countenance, if necessary, such acts. Where power and its attendant riches are so frequently the road to ruin, is it not surprising they should be so much sought after? Yet never was there a people more eager in their pursuit than the Moors. This in my opinion is principally the result of that excess of luxury so remarkable in these Eastern people, which grows up with them from their infancy and requires great sums to answer its demands and which, at any rate or danger, must be met.

This, however, it must be observed, is only the lot of a very small part of the inhabitants of this extensive country, the rest being rather miserably poor. Notwithstanding the richness of the soil, the exactions of their lords are so great as to leave them little more than the bare necessaries of life which, where food is so cheap, amount to surprisingly little. This state of poverty which the peasants are kept in frequently reduces them to the utmost misery, for, as they are obliged to be satisfied with their daily bread, a bad season puts it out of their power to get even that small pittance that, at best, is all they can afford. Then scenes of the greatest distress are common, many dying for real want and others selling their children to supply the craving calls of nature, often for the small value of about half a crown.

Thus are the greatest advantages of nature thrown away, if we ourselves do not improve them. Much better by all accounts was this country when in the hands of its original inhabitants the Gentoos, and we have the greater reason to credit this report by the fact that they are still a more industrious, ingenious, and innocent set of people than the Moors, for they are even to this day the principal and almost chief hands in carrying on the several manufactures and cultivation of the land.

In many instances there is an observable difference between the Gentoos on the coast of Coromandel and those in Bengal. That seemingly public-spirited institution of *choultries*, so numerous in those parts, is not to be found here. But in nothing is the difference more conspicuous than in the apparent want of any considerable place of worship. In the other parts of India that have fallen under my observation, those are the kinds of building in which they spare neither cost nor labour. Although in Bengal they may be remiss in this particular, however, they are much stricter observers of most of the considerable tenets of their religion than are the others. A temple called Jaggurcnat [Jaganath], similar to the Muhammadan Mecca, is situated on the coast near Vizagapatam [200 miles away], and most Gentoos never neglect going once in life—though it is a considerable distance from many parts of the province—and contributing to that considerable revenue which the priests there enjoy. It is said that they lay it out in feeding twenty thousand souls daily.

Those austerities which the Brahmins are so remarkable for are more frequently heard of here than in other parts. Many are the castes that never eat anything that had animal life in it. Others go in all seasons naked, from whence they are called Gymnosophists, and are held in the greatest esteem especially by the [female] sex who are often, by the prayers of these good men, relieved from the insupportable misfortune of barrenness. In short, many are the customs observed here. But the following ones, as they are very extraordinary and as I have been eye-witness of them, I shall particularise.

Some time in the month of April they celebrate a remarkable holiday, when the people assemble in great crowds on some plain in or near each town or village. Several poles are erected about thirty feet high, on the tops of which are laid others that turn on a swivel. At each extremity is a rope. To one is fixed a couple of iron hooks, in length about six inches, and at the other is a weight. Induced by a religious motive, multitudes offer themselves to the following severe discipline. The two forementioned hooks are thrust one on each side of the fleshy part of their back and a rope is put round their waist to bear part of the weight of the body. They are then hoisted up by the help of the weight at the other extremity twenty feet from the ground, are there twirled about for the space of three or four minutes, then let down. The irons are dragged out and a little fine mortar is put on each wound. Never in all this operation, which is none of the most gentle, do they make any noise or show the least sign of pain. One man has no sooner gone through this ceremony than another offers, and so on for the whole day. The intention is, by account, to expiate former sins and to render their deities propitious.

Another no less extraordinary religious custom is their destroying (or doing what is similar to it) those who according to the opinion of their doctors are past the power of medicine to recover. When that is the case, the relations and friends carry the person down to the river side where they wash him, and then, pouring some muddy water in his mouth, leave him there until death or his legs carry him off. The latter results from that efficacy which all the Gentoos imagine to be in the water of the Ganges; if the sick can recover, it will effect his cure. As it so seldom answers their expectation, I am surprised their eyes have not yet been opened. This would certainly save the lives of many, as it has been known for some of these poor wretches to be taken up by a European physician and to recover.

But of still a more extraordinary nature is that most in-human custom of the women burying or burning them-selves with their deceased husbands. It is such that had I not been witness of it I could scarce give credit to it. Being told there was a woman to be buried alive, I and several gentlemen all equally prompted by a spirit of curiosity, repaired to the appointed place, which was close to Calcutta. There we found a couple of women warming themselves over a small wood fire close to the river. The destined—or, more properly, voluntary—victim of this most unnatural custom seemed to be about forty years of age, clean in her dress and apparently very calm and composed in her mind, no way ruffled by any violent agita-tions yet unalterably determined to be buried with her husband. We used all the persuasion we could think of to dissuade her from her resolution, offered her a consider-able sum of money even to defer it till the next day, but got no other answer than that life was not worth keeping now her husband was gone, and that she would follow him and she hoped be with him that night. As persuasion would not do and violence might be dangerous to make use of, we let her proceed. This she did in the following manner. The corpse of her husband being laid on the mud near the hole it was to be buried in, and close to the river, she sat herself by it for a few minutes, seemingly in a pen-sive mood, and then rose and lit four or five lamps which she placed near the body. After this she mixed some rice and plantain in an earthen plate. Now a Brahmin, or one of the heads of the deceased's caste, read something which she seemed to repeat with attention. She then washed the corpse, and a small bundle of straw being lit and given in

L

her hand, she walked three times with it round the body with the greatest firmness and resolution although it was no easy task with the mud up to mid-leg. Again the priest repeated something, at which time, the lighted straw going out, she blew it up again. So composed were all her actions! Their prayers being ended, she put the fire to the beard of her husband. While she was performing this, some of the standers-by stuck the lamps in the mud round the grave and threw in the rice and plantain. Then the body was laid in the hole in a fitting posture, and she immediately followed it without the least alteration, no tremor of nerves nor agitation in her countenance. With a composure and steadiness scarce to be credited, she was helped down into the grave. A child of hers that was present, about twelve years old (in whom even at that age custom had so far got the better of nature that it was in no way moved at the loss of a mother—nay, even desired that she *should* be buried), was the first to throw a lump of mud on her, and the rest of the relations present then covered her as best they could. At first they set up a momentary cry, which was too short to prevent hearing any complaint the poor wretch might have made, but she never uttered any nor made the least groan.

As to the custom of burning, I have not seen it performed, but I had the following relation from a gentleman of undoubted veracity who, having the command of a considerable fort on the coast of Coromandel, was requested by some of the natives to allow the wife of a deceased Brahmin to burn herself with the corpse of her husband, it being customary on the coast in all districts belonging to the English to ask leave of the commanding officer. He, doubting the truth of what he heard concerning that custom, granted their petition. When all was ready, they came to acquaint him that the ceremony was then going to be performed. He attended them, and saw the designed sacrifice, who was a middle-aged woman of a comely person, with a steady composure in her countenance, conversing with a great deal of coolness with the relations and friends that encompassed her. She had not the least appearance of being intoxicated by any kind of draught, but even if she had been it would have had time to work off in the length of the march from her abode to the place of burning, which was about two miles. When they arrived at the pile, which consisted of a heap of sticks about two feet in height, the corpse was laid thereon and, after she had taken leave of all about her, and given some flowers to the commanding officer with that same composure as she had maintained all along, she lay down close to the corpse, one arm under his head. They then strewed some brushwood on them both and set fire to the whole. As long as she could speak, she continued conversing with those near her and never cried nor groaned the whole time, no noise being made elsewhere which would have prevented such exclamations being heard. The officer, who had intended preventing the last act, was deterred by the resolution and willingness with which she followed her husband and by the fear of irritating the vast concourse of people assembled on the occasion.

Women are not obliged to follow either of these customs, but if once they say they will leave their houses with that intent and afterwards retract, they are then held in greatest contempt, which is attended with the loss of their caste and their abandonment by all their family. To do it is reckoned a most meritorious action and very pleasing to their deities, and those who perform it with resolution are held in the greatest esteem.

This custom, according to report, has taken its rise from one no less inhuman, that of the women poisoning their husbands. To prevent this, a better expedient could surely not be thought of! At first the deed must have been by compulsion, but afterwards, probably, long use and superstition made it regarded as a good action and it has therefore been continued. Thus does custom, assisted by superstition, work on great and resolute minds, minds that in the paths of virtue would be capable of the most sublime heroism. But though the former may push them on to the act, it must be the latter—joined to a thorough certainty of future life—that enables them to perform it with that extraordinary, nay, almost incredible, resolution. Strong indeed it must be to render them so insensible to that dread of death which nature seems to have implanted in all its creatures. Is it not surprising that the grossest idolatry should give them that conviction which many more enlightened people have not?

There are other castes of the Gentoos that neither bury nor burn but throw their corpses in the river, which occasions in many places a pestilential air, but it soon disappears through the work of the innumerable swarms of jackals, vultures and kites which this country abounds with. How much to be admired are the dispensations of providence, which, even in these small particulars, has provided for the necessities of each climate! Here, where the warmth immediately putrefies every kind of filth, infection would certainly be the consequence were it not for the quantity of these animals.

The Moors who now are masters of this country are all Muhammadans of the sect of Ali, in general a lazy, idle set of people much addicted to their pleasures. Their principal towns correspond with their dispositions, being mean and dirty, and even Murshidabad, one of their most considerable, justly deserves that description. The nabob's palace, which is much the largest building, is made distinguished only by its extent. It has no elegance of architecture nor symmetry of parts. All is a heap of low apartments with a great number of little courts and gardens, without any order or disposition in the whole. There are a few large saloons, or more properly, open piazzas, that have a tolerable elegant appearance and are the only things I have seen in any of their buildings which deserve the least notice. In these places they receive their company and pass most of their time. The buildings are open and contrived entirely for coolness. It is the jealous disposition of the Moors that occasions their low and prison-like way of building; they thus foolishly attempt to restrain a sex which baffles their utmost skill, for even in the strictest seraglios they gratify their most wanton passions. Opposition and confinement only increase this, for they thereby prove they have a right to liberty equal to ours, and that reason and a sense of duty are the best and only guards for free-born creatures.

The rest of this town, except for a few houses belonging to the chief men, is made up of cabins which extend for above five miles on either side of the river and two in breadth. It is as full of inhabitants as it can hold. Indeed, all of this country through which I have passed is well peopled, which is easily accounted for by the fact that they have no settlements to drain them nor no wars to destroy them. They frequently take the field, but their battles are soon decided and with very little bloodshed.

The Moors are allowed by their religion to have as many wives and concubines as their fortune can maintain. But the Gentoos, as far as I could learn, think one fully sufficient for a man's happiness. They marry her at eight or nine years of age or younger, from which time the girl is kept close at home with the mother until she is of an age to cohabit with her husband. Then she is conveyed to him with great ceremony and the marriage is concluded. These women are reckoned virtuous, and though they do not all bury or burn with their deceased husbands yet they never marry a second time. The respect of children for their parents is very great. At no time do they throw off that strict submission to their will which nature, strengthened by reason, makes the right of dutiful parents and the pleasure of their children. Family connexions are here a most sacred tie, and there are few instances of one going in want when any of the rest have wherewithal to supply him. On the whole, they seem a much better set of people than their conquerors, retaining more of that charming native simplicity and innocence which probably, in earlier times, was the happy lot of the whole world. Both men and women are handsome, their dress much the same as what is worn on the coast of Coromandel, genteel and becoming.

As nothing contributes more to civilising a people than rational and sensible amusements, so is there no truer way of forming a judgement in that respect than by examining what that of each nation consists of. Little to the advantage of the Moors are those of their entertainments which have fallen under my observation. Colonel Clive and the officers of his guard were invited by the nabob at Murshidabad to a play, which we concluded—as it was being given by the prince of the country for the entertainment of a man to whom he owed his present grandeur —would be no bad test to judge from. It consisted of several different acts, with dancing between. Each seemed a detached piece, intended, as far as I could learn, to discourage vice and folly. Yet it was done in so rude and indecent a manner as rather to stir up the lewdest passions. The actions and countenance were very expressive, giving an insight into their meaning without the help of words. That act which struck me most was one intended to show the bad effect of giving ear to flattery, and the ridiculous figure people of low fortunes and little education make when they ape the ceremony of their superiors. In order to express this, two men, meanly dressed, appeared on the stage, one acting as the guest of the other. At their first accosting, they go through all the excesses of ceremony which the mimics of true good breeding generally fall into. A buffoon is then introduced to divert these gentlemen, and pleases them each in turn so well by his flattery that he gets for recompense their turbans. He continues to pursue the same strain and is frequently rewarded with some part of their dress. Now all they have left are their drawers, which one last effort of this soothing flatterer makes them strip off, leaving nature without disguise. Here was apparently the height of the jest for all the court, which consisted mostly of about sixty or seventy women. The moral was well chosen for a prince just then ascended to the throne, and, had the last part been left out, might have promised more polite entertainment to follow. But the other acts were still more indecent, providing high amusement for all present except those for whom the entertainment was given. Thus does this prince pass most of his evenings. We were afterwards present at several others but found them all in the same strain.

A more agreeable diversion which they are very fond of is going on the water. They have vessels well adapted for that purpose, called *boliahs*, which are rowed by twenty and sometimes more men with paddles, and go stern foremost. In the stern there is a pretty covered place for three or four to lie in accordance with the Eastern custom. Between that and where the boatmen sit is a small space where there is generally a buffoon who sings and dances for the amusement of those in the boat. There are a couple of rings to each paddle which, with no unpleasing effect, they make jingle to the time of what he sings. Besides these vessels there are others called snakes, from their being upwards of thirty feet in length and not, in the greatest breadth, above five. These are rowed by thirty and frequently more oars and go at a prodigious swiftness, but they are dangerous if it is not very calm, as their great length and very little breadth makes them liable to overset. They do not carry above two besides the boatmen, in a little covered place astern. In the month of July, some hundred of these different vessels come down from Patna for the nabob's amusement, and I believe serve him in collecting part of his tributes. Then they afford a very pretty show, their tops being ornamented with different coloured cloths, many embroidered with gold and silver, with fine carpets to lie on, and a great variety of streamers. They parade and row on the river in great order and state.

All these boats are fashioned for the Moorish method of lying down and the Europeans have improved on the plan and made most convenient ones for their own purpose, called *budgerows*, that have generally two pretty apartments in them, one for lying and the other for eating in. But neither are these suitable for any navigation but on smooth water, their stern being very high and therefore dangerous in wind or a rough sea. All our European gentlemen make their progress to the different settlements up the river in one of these kinds of boats.

This country has all the different kinds of animals that are to be found on the coast, with the addition of a great number of tigers that frequently do infinite mischief. As they generally keep near the river side, they have many opportunities of picking up boatmen who, mooring at night close to the bank, fall asleep and thereby give the animals time to seize one or more before they can put themselves on their defence. Once they have tasted human blood (for they only suck) they are remarkably fond of it, and I am told that they grow so bold as even to swim off to boats that lie some distance from the shore. There is a small kind of tiger somewhat like the leopard which is trained up to hunt deer. This amusement I have seen several times. The tiger [cheetah] is led hooded as near the deer as possible. Then they uncover his eyes and show him his game, when he creeps on his prey until it sees him. Then he pursues with great swiftness and generally overtakes it—though this appeared to me to be more the result of that animal's dread of its pursuer than of the pursuer's swiftness. If he finds the deer gaining much on him he stops and quietly returns to his keeper. When he seizes his prey he never lets go his hold but sucks there until he fills his belly. There is a smaller kind of animal about twice the size of a cat called a *shygosse* [lynx] which they train in the same manner for smaller game such as hares, goats and fowl. This creature is of the tiger kind and has ears placed like a cat's, about thrice as long, with hairs at the extremities resembling feathers.

The river Ganges abounds with alligators, some of a most enormous size. There was one brought to Colonel Clive upwards of twenty feet in length from his snout to the extremity of his tail and broad in proportion. It had a mouth furnished with a set of long, irregular teeth that could with ease take in half a man. They have four claws with which they can walk pretty fast. Their bellies are of a soft consistency and easily pierced, but on the back they have strong and thick scales that render them invulnerable to most weapons. Snakes are likewise of a great size here. One I saw measured eighteen feet in length and better than three in circumference. In the bellies of these animals are often found hares entire, with fowls and many other things. These are not the kind that are most venomous, for they are easily avoided as they move but slowly.

A very extraordinary animal abounds here called a muskrat, whose appellation comes from the smell it has of that perfume. This is so penetrating that, if it but pass over a bottle, the liquor in it will taste and smell strongly

M

of musk and is thereby rendered useless as it can never be cleared of it. They resemble our rats except that their tails are shorter and their eyes smaller.

The animals that supply the table—fish, flesh and fowls —are in great plenty. The mutton in particular is accounted extremely good. Bullock I have seen here much larger than any in Europe, commonly white. But these bear a high price, being held in great veneration by the Gentoos and used both by them and the Moors in drawing their carriages.

There is a fish particular to some parts of this river which is called the mango fish from its being in season at the same time as the fruit. It is as high-flavoured as anything of the kind I ever tasted.

Peas, cabbage, cauliflower, and many other kind of pulse belonging to our climate thrive here too, in as near perfection as in Europe. In a word, all kinds of eatables are plentiful and table indulgences may be, and I believe are, gratified better here than in any other part of India.

The Moors eat most kind of things that we do except swine's flesh, which they hold in great abomination. Their victuals are generally high-seasoned and palatable. Their common drink is sherbet but they are extremely fond of spirituous liquors and wine, which they will use to great excess notwithstanding it is expressly forbid them by their religion. The Gentoos never taste either, at least before an European, nor is there ever any example of their appearing intoxicated from liquor. That would be breaking one of the principal tenets of their religion and attended with the loss of their caste, which they seem to fear from dread of the pecuniary punishment which is generally inflicted on them before they recover it again. Their food is very simple, consisting principally of a kind of thick milk called *tier* [palm-toddy] and rice seasoned with spices. But they have a somewhat extraordinary particularity, which is drinking near half a pint of liquid butter, fasting. This they account extremely wholesome and it is practised by all the inhabitants. Their drink is milk and water, thus not varying in the least from that simple, primitive, and I believe wholesome food of their forefathers.

Nothing can better illustrate the cheapness of all kinds of things than the minute division of coins in Bengal, and the smallness of servants' wages. The rupee is the principal money of the country, of different value according to its age. Every year the Mughal coins new ones which are, for that year, called *sicca* rupees and are then the currency. In value they are about two shillings and tenpence. Those of the first year of his reign are called first *Suns*, the next second *Suns*, and so on as long as he fills the throne. They decrease in value as they are further removed from the present year. Those of a former reign are *sonaut* rupees and pass for nothing more than the real value of the silver. One hundred thousand rupees are a *lakh*, and one hundred *lakhs* a *crore*. There are also half and quarter rupees and a coin called an *anna*, sixteen of which make a rupee. There is also the *pice*, twelve of which make an *anna*. But these are not common. More common are the shells called *cowries*, which are got on the Maldive Islands. Their value varies, but in general they run from fifty to sixty pounds' weight for a *sicca* rupee, there being eighty *cowries* in each pound. Four cowries are called a *ganda*. For one, they can buy something in the market, and for a pound supply themselves with a tolerably good dinner. If necessaries were not so cheap it would be impossible for servants to live on the smallness of their wages, which is for the most of them, for food and clothes for their families as well as themselves, about two rupees per month.

I had like to have omitted a most essential article towards characterising the Moors and Gentoos, which is their extreme vanity and fondness for everything that can make them thought men of consequence. This vice, when they arrive at any command, leads them into a parade and show beyond what their income allows of, and contributes much to that oppression and poverty which the lower class of people labour under. Even the Europeans are obliged, in order to gain respect, to conform in this particular to the failing of these people, which makes the expense of living amount very high and is the principal hindrance to the attainment of that which induces most Europeans to go to those distant regions—making a fortune. From the same principle proceeds the fondness this people have of affecting pompous titles, which is well exemplified in the following grant.

COPY of a grant made by the King of Pegu [in Burma] &cᵃ to the East India Company of a settlement on the continent near the Island of Negrais—
I the King of the Burmans, King of Ava, Pegu, and Syriam, Siam, Cathsay, and Huan, Lord of the White and Red Elephants, and Lord of the Golden lance, Lord of mines and precious stones, gold, silver, iron, lead, copper &cᵃ, Lord of the gold and silver palace supported on pillars of gold set with precious stones, Lord of the Sun and Moon, of the Golden semiter, and King of my kingdom—
Out of my love and friendship to George the Second King of Great Britain France and Ireland &cᵃ &cᵃ I write the following.
Whereas in former times the English and Burmans were great friends, and continued so till the revolution occasioned by the rebellion of the Pegu-ers, which was the means of our separation for some time until the Honourable Company sent Mr Henry Brooke to settle a colony on my Island of Negrais which when I heard of their arrival it gave me great joy. By reason of our great distance I could not let you know the great love and

esteem I had for you, but as your people are now come to me I hope it will be perfected.

Now as the Honourable Company has sent Mr Henry Brooke to ask liberty of me for a piece of ground opposite to the town of Persaim of sufficient extent to build a Fort, Godowns [storehouses] &c^a and to build or repair their shipping, I have granted his request for the use of the Honourable Company and their Heirs for ever, and that Ensign John Dyer, and Doctor William Anderson have come to me on an embassy, accompanied with the Prince of Persaim, I have in the presence of the above Gentlemen, ordered the Prince to deliver the ground consisting of five hundred bamboos square (each bamboo being three Yards and a half). In testimony of which I have put my Royal signet as my assent thereto. I also grant them the full liberty of trade with all priviledges arising therefrom without paying any duties provided they have the Honourable Company's pass.

But if the Honourable Company will send me any present of Guns or warlike stores it would be very acceptable.

As we are friends now we must deal with one another with the honour of Kings, and supply me with what I may want from your Kingdom as you may depend on my supplying you with whatever you may want from mine. And I further desire that you with your Sons and Heirs may live in unity and friendship with me and my Sons and Heirs for ever. Written at Dagon in the Year of the Burmans 1118 the 10th day of the Moon in the month Cachaung, and saturday of the week. In the English stile on the Wednesday of the 12th of May in the Year of our Lord 1756.—

How far the translation is just I cannot affirm, but it was given to me by the doctor mentioned in the grant.

The following letter, though of a somewhat different style to the former, is yet I think worth inserting, as it will give some little idea of the Eastern epistolary way of writing. One thing I must observe, that the name of God which is expressed by the first letter of their aphabet is always put at the top of the paper, and the sentence is left blank at the point where the word should come in. This proceeds from the high veneration they have for the Almighty, that his name shall not be preceded by any other word.

The Nabob
Letter to Colonel Adlercron received the 9th June 1755—
TO the Valiant and Brave man Colonel Adlercron The Thunderbold of War—the 22nd day of the Moon 1168 of Mahomet—
I received a great deal of pleasure from the advantageous character which Captain Caillaud gave me of you, and I hope [God] will daily strengthen you in your good disposition. As a friend I make bold to send you four pieces of cloth, which I hope you will accept of. Pray continue to give me news of your health and Welfare—I can say no more.
P:S: By hearing of your character of bravery and conduct I have given you a title agreeable thereto: and have sent you a Chop [seal] accordingly—I wish [God] may give you success—
(Added in the nabob's handwriting)
I am much pleased with you, and desire you will continue a correspondence.

Most of their letters end in that laconic manner, 'I can say no more' or 'What can I say more'. The Chop is a ring on which is cut in Persian characters the title the nabob pleases to confer, and is esteemed one of the greatest favours.

Different as the customs and manners of mankind are over the face of the earth, yet how they resemble in essentials. Go where you will, you find the idea of a Supreme Being universal, and a firm belief in futurity implanted in almost every breast. Virtue is esteemed, and vice in general hated, and there is a strong indication that all have proceeded from the same great source of goodness, though time, place and intercourse have made different modifications. Trade not only transfers the manufactures of one nation to another, but likewise its vices, from whence I presume it will be found true that the towns of the greatest commerce are the most vicious, and therefore unfair places to make conclusive observations from in that respect.

I must own that, for my part, what I have seen of these distant regions has given me great satisfaction, from the many manifest signs of a paternal goodness diffused to all in equal proportion—not, as the too universal erroneous prejudice would induce us to think, confined to a span of earth and a handful of people.

I conclude with an excellent observation of Lord Orrery's. 'Perfection in every attribute is not indeed allotted to particular men: but, among the whole species, we discover such an assemblage of all the great, and amiable virtues, as may convince us, that the original order of nature contains in it the greatest beauty.'

GLOSSARY

of leading historical characters mentioned in the text

ALIVARDI KHAN (?1676–1756). Nawab of Bengal from 1740 —when he defeated his predecessor in battle—until his death in 1756. The first ten years of Alivardi's reign were devoted to fighting the Marathas, a warrior race from central India who were intent on seizing control of the north as it slipped from the failing grasp of the Mughal emperors. His attitude towards the English merchants in his territory was strict, and he took firm measures to curtail the use—and frequent abuse—of the privileges granted to them by the Mughals.

ARCOT, NAWAB OF (1717–1795). Muhammad Ali Khan, Nawab of the Carnatic from 1749 until his death. His accession to the 'nabobship'—as Corneille calls it—was challenged by Chanda Sahib, backed by the French, but Muhammad had English support. Clive (*q.v.*) took Arcot on his behalf in 1751, and he was ultimately recognised by the French in 1763. The case of 'the Nabob of Arcot's debts' was one of the great financial scandals of the eighteenth century. Muhammad Ali contracted vast debts to the East India Company and to the many adventurers who frequented his court, and assigned the revenues of various districts to meet them. Attempts were made, in treaties in 1763, 1781, 1785, 1787 and 1792, to arrange some method of liquidating the debts, but the Nawab died without any effective solution having been reached. In 1801, the East India Company took over the government of the Carnatic.

BUSSY-CASTELNAU, CHARLES JOSEPH PATISSIER, MARQUIS DE (1718–1785). French officer. He gained ascendancy for the French at Hyderabad, and in 1757 seized Vizagapatam and other English factories. In 1758 he was recalled by Lally, the new French governor-general at Pondicherry, and in 1760 was taken prisoner at the battle of Wandiwash where the English, under Eyre Coote (*q.v.*), were victorious.

Bussy is said to have made a large fortune during his career in India.

CAILLAUD, JOHN (1724–1812). British officer. Fought at Fontenoy and Culloden. Was commissioned by the East India Company in 1752 and joined Stringer Lawrence—'Father of the Indian Army'—at Trichinopoly in 1753. In 1759 he was appointed to the chief military command in Bengal and went to Calcutta, where he took a prominent part in deposing Mir Jafar (*q.v.*) before returning to Madras in 1761. Five years later, he was appointed commander-in-chief in succession to Stringer Lawrence. He returned to England in 1767. Caillaud's sister—and heiress—married Corneille's younger brother, Edward.

CLIVE, ROBERT (1725–1774). Arrived in India in 1744 as a 'writer' in the East India Company's service. His military talents first emerged at the siege of Pondicherry in 1748, and were confirmed in his seizure of Arcot in 1751 and the success with which he defended it against a siege by the superior forces of Chanda Sahib. After further successes, including the defeat of a French army near Trichinopoly, Clive returned to England in 1753. When he went back to India in 1756 as a lieutenant-colonel in the Company's army, Clive was immediately involved in the events chronicled in Corneille's book. But Corneille's military summary can give little hint of the complex diplomatic negotiations which led to Clive's alliance with Mir Jafar (*q.v.*) and the defeat of Siraj-ud-daula (*q.v.*). After Plassey, Clive became governor of Bengal. In England again between 1760 and the end of 1764, he was made Baron Clive of Plassey, became M.P. for Shrewsbury, and was awarded the K.C.B. He returned to Bengal as governor and commander-in-chief in 1765, when the Mughal emperor also gave him authority to administer the civil government and collect the revenues of Bengal, Bihar and Orissa. Clive's sweeping administrative reforms soon led to great discontent in the English Company, and when he finally returned to England in 1767 he himself was virulently attacked and his administration became the subject of a parliamentary enquiry. Clive was found to have rendered great service to his country but, worn out by ill health and depression, he took his own life in 1774. Clive's remark that he was astonished at his own moderation was not as nonsensical as the size of the fortune he made might suggest. He could have made much more.

Clive has been called an empire-builder without scruples. But, as Mountstuart Elphinstone, the great Indian administrator, wrote: 'In a life spent amid scenes of blood and suffering, he has never been accused of a single act of cruelty.' For this alone, much can be forgiven him.

COOTE, EYRE (1726–1783). First arrived in India at the same time as Corneille and was promoted captain in 1755. After Plassey he returned to England but was soon gazetted as lieutenant-colonel of the 84th regiment and returned to India in 1759. He defeated the French at Wandiwash and again at Pondicherry in 1761, after which the power of the French in India collapsed. Ultimately, after a further spell in England during which he was M.P. for Leicester, received a knighthood, and progressed upwards in military rank, he became commander-in-chief in India in 1777.

DRAKE, ROGER (1722–?). Arrived in India in 1737. He became president of the Council and governor of Calcutta in 1752 by right of seniority. Drake was not popular with his fellow merchants, for his character was weak and indecisive and his occasional attempts to stand firm were distressingly ill-timed. When Calcutta was about to fall to Siraj-ud-daula (*q.v.*), Governor Drake fled, leaving the final stand to others. His desertion resulted in dismissal by the Directors of the East India Company, after which he vanishes from history.

DUPLEIX, JOSEPH FRANCIS (1697–1764). After a profitable early career in India, Dupleix became governor of Pondicherry in 1741 and director-general of all French factories in India. Determined to create an empire, he decided to use Indian forms of government. He surrounded himself with magnificence, lived in oriental fashion, and was recognised by other Indian rulers as one of themselves. Dupleix was the first European to discover that Indian troops trained in European military science and led by European officers had overwhelming advantages against the disorganised rabble that constituted the native armies of India. His battles were many and often successful, though he was defeated by Stringer Lawrence and Robert Clive (*q.v.*). The Compagnie des Indes, complaining that Dupleix' constant scheming and fighting were ruinously expensive and detrimental to trade, sent Godeheu (*q.v.*) to supersede him and investigate his accounts in 1754. Godeheu refused to reimburse Dupleix for his private expenditure on behalf of France, and Dupleix returned to France in the same year. He died in comparative poverty ten years later.

GODEHEU, CHARLES ROBERT (*c.* 1710–?). A member of the French council at Chandernagore prior to 1741, and then a director of the Compagnie des Indes in France. He was sent out in 1754 to supersede Dupleix (*q.v.*), conclude peace with the English, and examine Dupleix' accounts. Godeheu brought about Dupleix' final ruin by rejecting his claims for repayment of sums advanced out of his private means as well as by the tenor of his reports on Dupleix' work. In his negotiations with Saunders (*q.v.*), Godeheu reversed Dupleix' policy and gave in on nearly all the points at issue. He returned to France in 1755.

MIR JAFAR (1691–1765). Commander-in-chief of the forces of Alivardi Khan (*q.v.*) and of his successor Siraj-ud-daula (*q.v.*). With the support of the English East India Company and the great Hindu bankers, the Seths, he was installed as Nawab of Bengal, Bihar and Orissa after the battle of Plassey in 1757. Within two years, however, he was found intriguing with the Dutch to expel the English from his territory, and the English deposed him in 1760. His son-in-law, Mir Kasim, who replaced him, in turn found himself at odds with the Company, and in 1763 Mir Jafar was restored to power and reigned quietly until he died of leprosy shortly afterwards.

PIGOT, GEORGE (1719–1777). Went to Madras in the East India Company's civil service in 1737 and rose steadily to the governorship of Madras in 1755. He was made a baronet in 1764 and, in the following year, resigned from the Company's service and returned to England where he became M.P. for Wallingford and Bridgnorth, and was made an Irish peer. Returning to Madras in 1775 as governor and commander-in-chief, he set about repressing malpractices. Disputes arose between himself and his Council, which resulted in Pigot suspending two members of Council and ordering the arrest of the commandant. The Council retaliated by arresting Pigot himself and imprisoning him until the Court of Directors in London passed judgement. The Court ruled that he should be restored to the governorship, but should immediately resign. In the meantime, however, Pigot had died in confinement. Four members of the Council were later tried in England for his arrest and were fined £1000 each.

POCOCK, GEORGE (1706–1792). After a successful early career in the Navy, he was sent out to India in 1754. He became rear-admiral in 1755 and second-in-command to Admiral Watson (q.v.) whom he succeeded in 1757, holding the command until 1759 and fighting two inconclusive naval engagements with the French off the Coromandel coast. After his return to England in 1760, Pocock was knighted and promoted admiral. His last exploit was the taking of Havana in 1762, after which, in 1766, he retired from active service.

RENAULT, PIERRE (dates uncertain). Chief of the French settlement at Chandernagore at the time of its fall to the English in 1757. He was taken to Calcutta, but released after Plassey. Renault next commanded in South India, but was again defeated by the British in 1760, and was thereafter court-martialled and cashiered.

SAUNDERS, THOMAS (c. 1716–?). Began in the Company's service in 1732 as a 'writer' at Madras and rose by 1749 to be chief at Vizagapatam. In 1750 he became governor of Madras, although located at Fort St David. His government was reestablished at Madras itself in 1752, where Saunders remained until he resigned the governorship and sailed for home in 1755.

SIRAJ-UD-DAULA (1736–1757). The son of Zaid-ud-din, favourite nephew of Alivardi Khan (q.v.). Mirza Muhammad, as the boy was originally named, became impatient for Alivardi's death and his own accession to the throne, and rebelled in 1750. Despite this, Alivardi officially adopted him in 1753 as his son and heir and he was thereafter known by the honorific title of Siraj-ud-daula, 'the lamp of the state'. He acceded as Nawab in 1756, by which time his mind was already affected by acute alcoholism. Siraj-ud-daula was violent and capricious by temperament. Prejudiced against the English Company because he feared the growth of their power, he also believed they were conspiring with his rival to the throne, and was avaricious of their wealth. Their actions in no way soothed his fears. His defeat and death followed only fifteen months after his accession.

WATSON, CHARLES (1714–1757). Joined the Navy in 1728 and had reached the rank of rear-admiral by 1748. His career in India—which is adequately chronicled in the course of Corneille's book—was successful and marred only by his constant differences with Clive (*q.v.*), whose subterranean diplomacy did not accord with Watson's concept of honourable dealing. He died from the effects of the climate in 1757.

WATTS, WILLIAM (1718–?). Chief of the English settlement at Kasimbazar. He was captured there by Siraj-ud-daula (*q.v.*) and carried off to witness the attack on Calcutta, although he was afterwards released. Watts was soon appointed to the Select Secret Committee formed to manage the Company's affairs in Bengal, when this 'helpless, poor and innocent man'—as Siraj-ud-daula had described him—played a crucial part in the negotiations with Mir Jafar (*q.v.*) which were to lead to Siraj-ud-daula's downfall. In 1758, Watts superseded Drake (*q.v.*) as president at Calcutta, but shortly handed over the charge to Clive (*q.v.*). Perhaps irrelevantly, it may be noted that Watts' grandson became the second Earl of Liverpool, prime minister of Britain from 1812 until 1827.